Love is the Link

Love is the Link

A Hospice Doctor Shares Her Experience of Near-Death and Dying

Pamela M. Kircher, M.D.

Published for the Paul Brunton Philosophic Foundation by

Larson Publications

International Standard Book Number (paper): 0-943914-76-0
Library of Congress Catalog Card Number: 95-78976

Published for the Paul Brunton Philosophic Foundation
by Larson Publications
4936 NYS Route 414
Burdett, NY 14818 USA

02 01 00 99 98 97 96 95

10 9 8 7 6 5 4 3 2 1

DEDICATION

THIS book is dedicated to the men and women who have shared their stories with me over the years. Our hearts and minds have touched as we have shared the deep mysteries of life. Details of their lives have been modified to preserve their privacy, but the essence of their stories has been maintained so that those who read the book will have the opportunity to share as much as possible in their experiences. May we all be blessed by the sharing!

CONTENTS

All this talk and turmoil and noise and movement and desire are outside the veil. Within the veil, there is silence and calm and rest.

Bayazid-Al-Bistami

FOREWORD

⇥ IT has been my good fortune to have known Pam Kircher—an exceptionally kind and spiritual person—since she was a resident in family practice. It was not until some years later that I learned she had a childhood near death experience (NDE).

Dr. Kircher is unique, in that her life experience encompasses virtually the whole field of near death studies. She is herself a near death experiencer. She is a physician and, more importantly, a hospice physician. She has led a spiritually oriented group investigating the meanings of NDEs. These qualifications enable her to compare and provide insights into virtually all facets of the NDE and related phenomena.

Love is the Link is a distillation of all this experience. In a single volume, with compelling and illuminating examples, Dr. Kircher deals not only with acute NDEs (the type most commonly reported) but also with "deathbed visions," the NDEs of terminally ill patients. Next she discusses rarely reported negative NDEs in a straightforward but loving manner. Then she goes on to integrate near death experience with the larger subject of mystical experience as well—which, according to recent polls, 40–50% of Americans and Europeans report having.

While she is well read regarding the scientific investigation of NDEs and related religious and mystical topics, Dr. Kircher doesn't focus on the now well documented scientific-clinical approach. Instead, she offers a spiritual look into near death experience—one that brings us to our "source" without dogma.

Briefly put, Dr. Pamela Kircher knows near death experience from the inside out and the outside in. Her own compelling childhood NDE and her vast experience as a hospice physician make her unique in the field.

—KEN R. VINCENT
author, *Visions of God from the Near Death Experience*

PREFACE

᷒ THIS book is in two parts. Part 1 is autobiographical. It describes
how I came to be so involved in near-death experiences. In it, I tell
as honestly as possible what my motivations and values have been in
this work. Value changes as a result of an NDE have been reported
in many books and articles, but I thought that readers might be
interested in seeing how a person who has had an NDE goes about
making choices in the world.

The story of my own NDE adventures from 1988–1994 imparts
something of the flavor of the general changes in attitude in the U.S.
toward NDEs over that six-year period. It was a historic time, as people
seemed to awaken almost overnight to the presence of the mystical
in their lives.

Part 2 presents stories I have heard from people in my work and
ideas I have developed as a result of them. My ideas are not meant
to be definitive ones on the topic, merely some ideas that I have
developed after hearing these stories. I invite you to mull them over
and develop your own opinions and ideas. If reading an autobiographical sketch by a physician/near-death experiencer doesn't appeal to you,
please skip directly to Part 2.

PROLOGUE

◁ THE year was 1950. A six-year-old girl dressed for a Halloween party in her small middle-class home in Missouri. As she put on her costume, her throat was beginning to hurt. She hurried on to the party anyway, expecting much fun.

As she began bobbing for apples at the party, her throat was hurting so much that it was difficult to open her mouth. She stayed until the party was over, but felt worse with each passing moment.

During the night, she began developing a headache. By the next morning, she could barely swallow because of the pain.

At church that morning, she developed new symptoms. She stood to say the Lord's Prayer with her eyes shut, and found herself unsteady on her feet. She could no longer keep her balance. As the day wore on, the headache extended into a neckache as well and her neck became quite stiff.

Throughout the night, the pain was so intense that sleep was impossible. The little girl and her mother both stayed up all night, waiting for the morning when she would be taken to the doctor. As her hair was brushed that morning, the slightest movement of her neck was excruciatingly painful. The hair was very tangled after a night of tossing and turning, and the task of brushing it was difficult.

As soon as the doctor saw her, he was very alarmed: A leaking abscess around the tonsils had led to meningitis. He gave her an injection of penicillin and told her mother that she would either live or die, but that nothing more could be done—except to be very careful that she didn't jolt the abscess and cause it to leak more.

The frightened young mother carried her daughter into the house, with great care not to jar the abscess, and put her to bed.

The next thing the little girl experienced was suddenly, inexplicably, being in the corner of the room *near the ceiling,* and looking down at a little girl in the bed. She was not surprised or frightened, even though nothing in her solid Midwest background had prepared her for an out-of-body experience. She was totally without pain and in perfect peace. She had the strong sense that she was *surrounded* by God. She did not feel like a boy or a girl or a child or an adult. She experienced the essence of herself—the soul that had existed before she came into her body, and that would exist when this life was over. She felt strong and peaceful and totally connected with God. Looking down at the little girl in the bed, she was aware of the girl's pain and felt compassion for her. As she further contemplated the situation, she realized that *she* must be that girl, and then the experience ended.

❧ ❧

THAT little girl was me, and the experience totally influenced the paths that my life would take. Partly as a result of that experience, I have come to understand how tiny the distance is between the world we think we inhabit and the world of the Spirit.

Living from a strictly materialistic point of view is like being in a small anteroom that is plainly furnished with a wooden straight-backed chair, a simple wood table, and a small rag rug on the floor. The walls are painted off-white with one or two still-life fruit paintings on the walls. The room measures around seven by seven feet. Mostly, that is all that is noticed. Once in a while a curtain is noticed on one of the walls—but not much thought is given to it. Just occasionally, however, something draws attention to that curtain and it suddenly seems much more like gossamer than heavy cotton. If you focus on the curtain, a distinct sense arises that there may be something beyond it. At just that moment, a breeze may come "out of nowhere," blowing the curtain back ever so slightly, revealing a much different room just beyond the one currently inhabited. How can this be? The temptation is to look quickly away and return to the straight-backed chair and simple table, deliberately turning away from the curtain that reveals the totally unexpected.

But continuing to watch the curtain in the hope of another breeze is one way of approaching this new reality.

Perhaps another breeze doesn't come: you lose patience and your attention returns to the room. The "curtain experience" is forgotten—until the next breeze comes and, suddenly, your attention goes to the curtain again. It may hold so much interest that now your attention continues to be focused on it until the next breeze comes, and then the next, and the next.

With each breeze, the curtain floats aside to reveal just a bit more of the next room. The desire to see into the into the next room becomes an ever-increasing fascination. At some point, it may become so overwhelming that the curtain draws fully aside, perhaps creating a great deal of trepidation.

You see a huge drawing room with velvet walls, sumptuous easy chairs, a thick Oriental carpet, polished wood floors, a fire in a massive stone fireplace, soft lights, and gentle music. You can see a beautiful garden through the next room's large picture window. You enter this room and it feels like home; the ante-room quickly becomes a distant memory.

Gradually, though, sounds begin to emanate from the ante-room, drawing your attention back there. The clamor grows louder and, reluctantly, you return. The talk and activity and turmoil going on there now may have such power that the sumptuous room becomes a distant pleasant memory—perhaps even just a dream? Or you may be pulled simultaneously toward both the ante-room and the sump-tuous room, a sort of tug-of-war that drains your energy and creates the feeling of being pulled apart.

For some the sumptuous room is savored only on special occa-sions, with the full knowledge that it is always there. For others the curtain may be pulled aside and both rooms so easily used that they begin to feel like one room.

My near-death experience as a six-year-old child with meningitis was the first time for me that the breeze blew the curtain aside. As with all near-death experiences, it was quite a gust of wind: the sumptuous room was easily seen, never to be forgotten. Though my attention has frequently been focused on the ante-room, I have also watched the curtain often for other breezes and have not been disappointed. Through the last several years, while I have talked with hundreds of people who have had near-death experiences and worked with terminally-ill patients as a hospice physician, the curtain has stayed open much of the time. It has brought a sense of living in both worlds simultaneously—not in struggle, but in full appreciation of what each area has to offer.

This book is a sharing of what I have learned—both from my own experiences and from the experiences of many other people who have been drawn into the other room. Sit back and relax: maybe the curtain will blow aside for you as well, as you read about these experiences.

PART 1

My Experience with Near-Death Experiences and Hospice Work

❧ ❦

CHAPTER 1

How My Work with Near-Death Experiences Began

↦ AMONG the many books about NDEs, this one comes from the unique perspective of a family physician who also has had a near-death experience. In addition, for four years I cared for terminally-ill patients in a hospice setting. From 1989 through 1994, I gave some fifty lectures to a variety of groups including college classes, churches, professional societies (nurses, social workers, medical students, and physicians), and facilitated an NDE support group on a monthly basis.

What I have learned beyond a shadow of a doubt is that there is much more to existence than the things we routinely see, touch, and feel when aware of only our physical surroundings. Talking with many people over the years, I have found that most people have some events in their lives that indicate this to them, and that frequently they repress these experiences because they are beyond their understanding of how the world functions.

This need to suppress the memory of unusual experiences is particularly prevalent among physicians. Most are certain that they understand how the world works. Experiences like near-death experiences, the psychic ability to know one's time of death, or visitations from dead relatives simply don't fit into their framework of understanding.

When I began to consider talking about NDEs, it was with a great deal of trepidation. I remembered my own childhood NDE and had read a couple of books on the subject; but I did not personally know any other people who had had the experience. The books I had read convinced me that such stories were common enough that physicians should at least be aware of the possibility of such an experience during cardiopulmonary resuscitation.

Then, in late 1988, one of my family practice patients told me of his recent NDE when he underwent anesthetic complications during routine elective surgery. (He had been a patient of mine for several years and felt completely comfortable with me.) A very practical young engineer, he had been very puzzled when he found himself out of his body, watching the surgery, and then traveling down a tunnel toward a light. Perhaps the most surprising part was the incredible peace that he felt, although he had no belief system that would have supported such an experience.

I was able to reassure him that such experiences are quite common and also quite natural. I referred him to a couple of books on the subject, invited him to come back if he wanted to talk about it more, and sent him on his way to integrate the experience into his life.

When I was asked to give a case presentation to the Family Practice residents the following month, I chose to present his case. I felt that it would be important for these people to know that some of their patients would be having NDEs and that a receptive and informed family doctor could be enormously helpful. They were accustomed, however, to case presentations about unusual cases of renal failure, tumors, and so on at their noon conferences, so my talk would be a radical departure from the usual fare.

I prepared carefully with slides about frequency of occurrence, changes as a result of the experience, and various physiologic proposals (and why they didn't totally explain the phenomenon). As I prepared for the talk, I shared my fears that I would be totally rejected by my colleagues with a friend who was a computer programmer at a medical school. He said that it was the toughest audience I could pick for my first talk and that, after I had given this presentation, nothing else would ever be that difficult again! The years have indeed proved him right.

When the day arrived, I gave the slide presentation to the Family Practice residents and the faculty at the noon conference. When the lights went on and discussion began, I was enormously relieved. Faculty began telling of times when patients had told them of NDEs, although most of them had not known what to make of it at the time. They found it very helpful to know about the statistics and the changes commonly seen in people as a result of NDEs. Because the faculty was receptive, residents were willing to think of it as a possibility.

After the talk, hospital life went on much as it had before. I didn't get the sense that people were whispering about me behind my back, but I did get the sense that they mostly dismissed this new information; it simply didn't blend in with medicine as they knew it. For me, however, it was a watershed experience. I had had the courage to speak my truth, I hadn't died on the spot, and I knew that I would be speaking my truth more and more often as time went on.

⊰⊱

MY patient with the NDE was instrumental in my choosing to talk about NDEs, but there was a personal component to it as well. I had told no one about my own NDE. It felt like a gift from God that didn't need validation from other people to be real. Though I knew it had been a powerful presence in my life from that time onward, I didn't realize how powerful it had been in determining my life's path until I read Kenneth Ring's *Heading Toward Omega* in 1988.[1] As I read that book about value changes in people as a result of their NDEs, I suddenly understood how very powerful the experience had been for me. Because of my young age at the time of my NDE, I had no recollection of any value changes that occurred as a result of it.

However, as I read Ken's book, many things began to fall into place for me. He had done in-depth psychological interviews with 143 people who had undergone NDEs. The purpose of the interviews was to determine if the NDEs had any influence on their values or the course of their lives. He found that these people tended to become much less interested in material success and much more interested in helping people. They often changed professions from those that are more lucrative financially to ones that are more service-oriented, often at a markedly reduced income. They also became more interested in nature and observed a oneness in all of life that they had not been aware of before. There was also a great increase in interest in spiritual matters and the meaning of life.

As I read the book, I cried with tears of recognition. So many puzzling aspects of my childhood were suddenly made clear! I remember wanting to be a medical missionary when I grew up. My two heroes were Albert Schweitzer and Mahatma Ghandi. My sister and I alternated fantasy "Ghandi" and "Schweitzer" games with "Cinderella" and "Sleeping Beauty" games as we took turns changing the game of the hour.

I remember being totally appalled by teasing as a child. I could never understand why anyone would want to do that, as I could feel the emotions of the person being teased and it was extremely painful. I was fortunate not to have been the target of teasing, but, nevertheless, being in its presence in any form made me acutely uncomfortable; yet, I felt powerless to stop it.

I remember one girl in elementary school who was slightly retarded mentally and quite awkward. She also was rather short-tempered. When people teased her, she would strike out at them but, because she was so awkward, she would never hit them. They considered it quite a game, but she was continually upset and angry. I tried to avoid her pain until one day I was confronted with it directly.

We were in the same class. One day I was rushing to lunch and accidentally bumped into her as I hurried to get in line. Although I had only brushed against her, she looked as though I had struck her and immediately started hitting me with her little fists. The class started chanting, "Hit her back! Hit her back!" With that shouting in the background, I looked in her eyes and suddenly felt what her life must be like. She looked like a hunted animal. Everywhere she turned, she was attacked.

Ignoring the shouts and the flailing fists, I looked her straight in the eyes and told her that I would never hurt her on purpose. It was absolutely an accident. Slowly, she calmed down and stopped hitting me.

As I prepared to make my way to my place in line, I gently put my hand on her arm and again assured her that she could count on me to never hurt her. We both had tears in our eyes as we turned back to our places in line. That experience occurred many years ago, but I have never forgotten how it felt to be her. I can only hope that somehow the rest of her life went better than elementary school did.

During my childhood, church was one of my favorite places to be. Although we were Methodist, I really appreciated the Midnight Mass at my grandmother's Catholic church. The stained glass windows, incense, and quiet reminded me of the total peace that I had felt during my experience. I again felt surrounded by God. It was puzzling to me that I was more interested in the spiritual feeling of being in a church than in what was actually said. During those early years, I felt that God had made me defective by making me too sensitive to other people's feelings and that I had been given an NDE in order to remember my origins and my destination. I remember many times feeling such pity for people in pain and comforting myself with the wonderful knowledge of what lay ahead for them. When I read Ken Ring's book, though, I suddenly realized that my sensitivity was a result of the experience, not that the experience was necessary in order for me to be able to live in the world.

As I grew older, I found myself very interested in all of the world's religions. As a teenager, I read through the whole Bible while studying Thomas à Kempis and other mystical writers of all persuasions. This interest in spirituality in its many forms has persisted to this day. I am continually struck with the commonality of all religions under the superficial differences. It seems to me that the saints of all religions have more in common with each other than they do with people of their own religions who are only interested in the words, and who don't live the principles.

I have never been particularly interested in material possessions. This is another characteristic of people who have had NDEs, and one that puts them out-of-synch with many other teenagers. I remember, for example, trying to be interested in clothes in order to be part of the conversation as a teenager; but it was nearly impossible. This lack of concern for material possessions has been very helpful throughout my life, though. It has allowed me to have much more freedom than if I had cared about acquiring things. It was particularly helpful to me when I was a single-parent medical student whose only income was child-support payments that were privately arranged and not declared by a judge.

Another similarity that I share with other people who have had NDEs is a voracious interest in learning. I have had a passion for studying all of my life. I love to read and to learn new things. It is an absolute passion! On occasion, it even gets in the way of my fully participating in the more mundane tasks of daily living.

All of these ideas went through my mind as I read *Heading Toward Omega* in late 1988. Suddenly, many aspects of my childhood that I had puzzled over made perfect sense. I was simply an ordinary person with an NDE! As I experienced my own relief and gratitude, I knew that I wanted to help other people have that same feeling. It occurred to me that it would be helpful to share my experience and knowledge about NDEs with other people. The talk to the residents in January had not included my personal experience, just the literature and the case presentation from my patient. I felt that it was important to also share my own story with other people. Once I had made the decision to do so, opportunities were not slow in coming.

If I were to talk about my personal experience in public, I would first need to tell the people in my life about it. Although the experience had occurred in 1950, I had never told a single person about it. I first called my mother in Missouri to tell her my recollections. I shared with her what I remembered and explained to her that I hadn't told her at the time because I was afraid that she would be frightened and try to "fix" me in some way, while I was certain that it was normal and a gift from God.

After I described my NDE to Mom, I asked her if she was aware of a time when that might have happened. She said tearfully that she knew exactly when it happened. She had never told me about the illness because she didn't want me to think of myself as fragile and didn't want me to know how close to death I had come. But she remembered well the long weekend with the intensifying headache, stiff neck, and lack of balance. She then told me about the visit to the doctor's office, where I was diagnosed with a leaking abcess and she was told I might not survive the illness. We both laughed and cried about how we each had important pieces of the puzzle that we had kept secret in order to "protect" the other person. When we put them together, the experience made perfect sense.

When I told Mom about the typical changes in people as a result of the experience, she was very interested and said that it did help to explain a lot about my childhood. She wasn't surprised at all about the NDE and has been very supportive of my work since that day that we first talked.

The next person that I told about it was my husband. He appreciated that it was very significant to me, but remained skeptical about its commonness and general significance for some time. However, he knew that I felt a need to talk about it and supported my doing what I felt I needed to do.

Having shared my experience with my family and having resolved in my own mind to begin sharing my experience, I was now ready to begin the next phase of my life.

CHAPTER 2

Learning the Meaning of Commitment

⇥ FOR my first public talk, I chose to speak in Grace Hall at my church. I had many friends there and it felt like a "safe" environment. A hundred or so people were there and they were very interested. Afterwards, in the question-and-answer period, several people shared their experiences. It was a very positive experience for me: Even at that first talk, it was apparent that people have a lot more to say about their experiences than they can express in a few brief minutes.

From the beginning, I decided to talk about NDEs when asked, but not to seek out speaking engagements. It has been interesting how that has evolved through the years. Public speaking was difficult for me as a child and was never something that I had enjoyed doing before, but I now felt so strongly about the need for physician-NDE experiencers to speak out that my convictions outweighed my natural hesitancies. As the years unfolded, the experiences built on each other and what I was able to share increased exponentially. It was as though there were a plan, but certainly not one laid by me.

My promise to the Holy Spirit was that I would never say "No" to any request, no matter how many fears it brought up for me. In exchange, the Holy Spirit has guided me in gentle paths so that I was never too terrified as the challenges gradually built on each other as well; no one step seemed impossible.

I have also always prayed and meditated before each encounter and asked to be a vessel for the Holy Spirit, to be open in my heart and mind to each person present, and to say what is most helpful to the individuals listening at a given moment. For that reason, I have never prepared a "standard" talk that I always give, but have allowed myself to be guided day by day. I have found myself feeling much more relaxed as time has gone on, by virtue of both an increasing knowledge about NDEs and an increasing trust that the Holy Spirit will be there to provide just the right words at just the right time.

Although beginning the talks was a turning point in my life, it completed a phase of preparation that had begun two years previously. Throughout my life I had been interested in spiritual matters and was blessed to feel frequently quite connected with the Holy Spirit. I had attended the church since moving to Houston in 1975 to start medical school, but I had never been particularly involved with the inner workings of the church or anything other than Sunday services and occasional special lectures or workshops. In 1987 I was asked to serve on the Board of the church. In meditating on the meaning of that, I felt strongly that while I had been "satisfied" with my spiritual life as an individual, if I were going to think about guiding the church, I would need to deepen my spiritual practices.

Upon making this decision, two things come to me that were very helpful. One was an introduction to the *Course in Miracles*.[2] The other was a movie that inspired me to follow my spirit in spite of any inconveniences—an idea that began to captivate me.

I meditated about what it would mean in my life to totally follow my spirit. As soon as I meditated, I got the answer: "Give up one year's salary. It will help you to see if you love the practice of medicine as much as you think you do, and will give you the opportunity to really stretch your ability to be committed."

It so happened that we were incredibly short of space for our youth program at the church at that time, and that a building was available for purchase next door to our church. It was quite run-down and had recently been used as a large dance studio, but it was a good size and location for our needs. As it happened, my annual income was just about what was needed for a down-payment.

I asked my husband to see the movie that had inspired me and explained to him my need to further understand commitment. He knows me well and said that he would go along with the idea if I would be willing to stand in front of the congregation and tell them about my plans. Because I am a shy and private person, telling my story before a large group of people was much more terrifying to me than donating a year's income to the church. Nevertheless, I agreed to do it, and thereby learned some valuable lessons.

I had several preconceived notions about what might happen as a result of my doing this, none of which came true. First, I feared that people would think that I was crazy. In fact, people admired my conviction in the same way that I had admired the conviction of the people in the movie. I also thought that people would ask me for money, thinking that I was "an easy mark." In fact, no one did. Finally, I feared that people would follow in my footsteps and lead themselves to financial ruin. I was acutely aware that while we had always used my income, we were a family of two doctors; the reduction in income would be only moderately inconvenient, not devastating. In fact, people used their own good judgment and simply stretched a bit beyond what had been comfortable.

The year was a wonderful one. Because of my conviction, other people asked themselves how they could be helpful in the creation of the youth center. As a result, a team was formed to renovate the old building. Architects and engineers donated their time for the plans. Others helped first with the cleaning up and then with the building and finishing. Lovely original art work was donated, as well as all of the bathroom fixtures. There was a wonderful feeling of cooperation and giving as the building was completed over the next several months. We all got to feel the experience of commitment. We named the main room "Grace Hall" in memory of *Amazing Grace and Chuck* (the movie that had inspired me) and in memory of the grace that flowed through us all as we converted the building. It was an experience that we all wanted to remember and to share for a long time to come. So it felt especially fitting to me that my first talk about my own near-death experience would take place in Grace Hall.

In my private life, I initially was very careful with spending money because, frankly, I didn't know how we would manage. I just knew that I needed to experience total commitment. As the year went on, we somehow became quite comfortable on the new income and the reduction was hardly noticeable. In fact, from that day on we rarely used my income for daily expenses. We used it for future dreams. I also found that I continued to enjoy caring for patients, perhaps more than ever because I had a much stronger sense of being centered than I had ever had before in my life.

It was at the end of that year of total commitment that I gave my first talk on NDEs. Having followed my own convictions with regard to the income had freed me enormously to follow my own inner guidance in many other areas of my life as well. Now I was ready, even though colleagues might think that I had "gone off the deep end" or question me as a scientist and physician.

CHAPTER 3

Beginning the Hospice Work

⇥ IN 1989, I began meeting with a small group of friends who had been studying the *Course in Miracles* for several years. Our goal was to be open and honest with each other as we really attempted to apply the teachings to our daily lives.

That association was a very powerful one for me because I have tended throughout my life to be caught up in what is "fair" and "getting justice done." Throughout that year these friends helped me to turn over my feelings of discomfort to the Holy Spirit and to perceive things in a different way. I began to see that what appears to be unfair and "not right," is often quite fair and right in the overall scheme of things—and that my part is to listen carefully to the Holy Spirit and follow my own inner guidance. I began to see life as a tapestry that is beautiful and perfect when seen in its entirety.

We each have our own threads to weave in that tapestry. From our personal perspective, we are much too close to individual events to guess at the perfection of the whole. Trust is required that we are weaving our thread right where it needs to be. That can only be done by spending time in silence and meditation so that we have an opportunity to hear our own inner guidance.

Life is not a random series of events that one meanders through until death. Each encounter is an opportunity to interact with love and grace. People who have undergone life reviews in NDEs tell of the importance of each moment. Each and every experience is relived. A person frequently feels not only his or her own feelings during the encounter, but also the feelings of the other person with whom one is interacting. "Chance" encounters in the grocery store line or in rush hour traffic are not random annoying events, but opportunities to create a more loving world. As I continued to study and to learn from other people, the world began to take on a depth and richness that I had been only dimly aware of before.

As I began to give talks in 1989, I realized that I had some questions that I would like to discuss with an expert so that I could be as helpful as possible. Consequently, I wrote a letter to Elisabeth Kubler-Ross, M.D., who had been caring for and writing about dying patients since the mid-sixties. I hoped for a phone conversation, but what I got was truly amazing.

As Elisabeth told me later, she literally had two rooms full of letters in her remote mountain home in Virginia. A couple of days after my letter arrived, she decided to answer a letter and went into one of the rooms and pulled *my* letter out. The letter explained how I was just starting to talk about NDEs and needed clarification on some points. She had her secretary arrange for me to visit her at her home. Because of the remoteness of the area, I would need to stay on the premises and she suggested that I stay a couple of days.

The opportunity of staying at Elisabeth Kubler-Ross' home was such an incredible gift that I wanted to be sure that I took full advantage of it. Consequently, I first attended a five-day workshop on "Life, Death, and Transition" conducted by people specially trained by her. The workshop's purpose was to assist people in the "externalization process": that is, to help them express suppressed painful emotions around grief. These five powerful days helped me to better understand her way of working with grief. I also met a woman there who worked with people with AIDS. We spent many valuable hours talking about how to care for dying people who wanted to live well while they were alive.

After the workshop, I made my visit to Elisabeth Kubler-Ross. She was a most gracious hostess who answered my questions and told me of her experiences well into the night. She had been with many dying patients, many of whom told her about NDEs. She validated my hunch that the understanding of NDEs is very crucial in our understanding of how the world functions all the time—not just when we are near death.

⊰⊱

AFTER that meeting, I continued to give talks throughout the Houston area. One particularly significant evening I had a discussion with a group of men with AIDS. Around fifty of us sat in a circle in a cozy room of the church and began talking to each other as people who had had NDEs. I shared my experience first and then, one by one, they began to share theirs. Because they were all so ill, most of them had been quite close to death at least once.

One man in his forties told of his experience as a boy during a childhood illness. He remembered well the feeling of peace and joy that he experienced during his NDE. That memory was what made it possible for him to go through the pain and ostracism that he was experiencing as a man with AIDS. He knew that when it was all over, he would be back in that place of perfect peace, surrounded by God.

Another man talked about how terrified he was of dying until he had his NDE in the intensive care unit. As a result of that experience, he was no longer afraid of dying. He was still angry about having the disease, but at least he wasn't afraid to die anymore.

Another person shared that his experience during an episode of a severe infection allowed him to let go of much of his anger about the disease itself. As a result of his life review, he felt that everything has a purpose, even AIDS. That was hard for some of his friends to hear, particularly those who had not been privileged to have an NDE.

Two men shared stories that were very similar. Each of them had been unconscious in an intensive care unit when seen by consultant physicians who gave advice and treatment for their complicated medical conditions. Each of them could describe the consultants in detail although these consultants had seen them only briefly and only when they were unconscious. They remembered not only what the doctors looked like, but also what they said. I have shared these stories with medical students on many occasions, so that they will be respectful of what they say in front of presumably unconscious patients.

As we shared with one another, it became evident that around 50% of the group had undergone an NDE at some time in their lives. I had never before been in a group of people with so many NDEs and was totally taken with the feeling of camaraderie that we had together even though our circumstances and backgrounds were so dissimilar. These men had been meeting weekly for some time and were close because of the severity of their illnesses, but they had not discussed NDEs with each other before. As we left, I heard small groups continuing to talk about NDEs, comparing the details of their experiences, but mostly talking about how significant they had been in their lives. I felt that the evening helped them to initiate an even deeper understanding of each other and hoped that such freedom to discuss NDEs would continue. There was such a peace among these friends as they briefly released the reality of their painful physical circumstances and allowed themselves to remember the reality of their NDEs.

⤙ ⤚

THROUGHOUT 1989, I continued to give occasional NDE talks. As I gave more talks, I became known as someone interested in the mystical. People began sharing all kinds of mystical experiences with me.

For example, one veteran shared an experience of having been saved by a quiet Voice that "told" him to remain in the tent in Korea as his group was leaving. Three times the voice said "Not now," and three times he hesitated. After the third time, he heard explosions outside the tent. He would have died if he had not followed the voice.

While I was definitely just learning about mystical experiences, it was becoming clear that there was a real need for a safe, accepting environment where people could come to talk about their NDEs and other mystical experiences. For that reason, I began facilitating a monthly meeting at the Unity Church of Christianity in November, 1989. People in the group found it useful to share similar stories with each other in an open, loving atmosphere. They found great comfort and practical support from others who had adjusted to life after an NDE.

As my interest and involvement in NDEs continued and intensified in 1989 and the beginning of 1990, the counseling aspect of my family practice moved toward more grief counseling. My background in NDEs and the Elisabeth Kubler-Ross workshop had spurred me to read more about death and dying. It seemed as though the needs of the counseling clients shifted as my own interests shifted.

At the same time that my spiritual life was intensifying, big changes were occurring in medicine. There was a burgeoning of HMOs at that time in Houston, and with it came an enormous increase in paperwork and difficulty in caring for people—so many administrative hassles! Once the patient and I had agreed on a course of action for a given problem, then we had to contact the HMO for permission. The HMO's phones were understaffed, and my employees began spending hours of each day waiting to get permission for obvious tests or procedures. The wait was always vastly inconvenient and sometimes it could be dangerous for the patient. If things were done without permission (even though they were clearly indicated), the HMO could refuse to pay.

Luckily, nothing tragic ever occurred; but it was a big worry to me, and this process made medicine not nearly as rewarding for me as it had been for the past eight years. As a family physician, I had been blessed to be involved in the care of generations within a family. Even in the big city of Houston, I had families where I had assisted a young woman through her teenage years, counseled her prior to her marriage, and was now caring for her children. Meanwhile, I had assisted her mother through menopause and the death of her father, for whom I had also cared. I loved being a family doctor, but the intrusion of big business was taking away the intimacy that I had so enjoyed with patients. As 1990 progressed, medicine no longer held the allure for me that it had once had.

In May, 1990, I went to bed one night feeling particularly oppressed by the big business aspect of medicine. I knew that something had to change for me, but I wasn't sure just what. As I went to sleep,

I prayed that I be given a solution to my dilemma or, at least, a direction that I should go. (I have found over the years that it is very helpful to say an intentional prayer over any problem as I go to sleep. It leaves my unconscious mind open to divine guidance.) At 2 A.M., I woke with a start and felt compelled to pull our monthly Harris County physicians' newsletter out of the trash and look at the classified ads. The first thing I saw was an ad for a physician at a local hospice. It seemed to make perfect sense.

As I reflected on the past three years, it was as if everything had prepared me for this work even though I didn't know at the time that I was being prepared. It seemed a natural next step in my life's work. The experience of giving away my income for a year had allowed me to taste the freedom of doing something dramatic and seeing that it was perfectly safe. Although giving up my practice of eight years would be a leap of faith, it seemed possible after three years of allowing myself to be led by my inner guidance. Contemplating the hospice possibility, I realized that to work with dying patients would be very helpful to me as well, as I was striving to understand more about the connection between life and death.

I interviewed with the hospice's medical director the following day. The hospice had instituted a nationwide search for a physician. Although the medical director knew of my work with NDEs, he hadn't thought to mention the position to me as I was a very popular, well-established family physician in the community. My qualifications were just what the hospice needed at that time and I was formally accepted for the position within a week or so.

May and June were spent closing my practice and finding appropriate physicians for each of my patients. The rest of the summer and early fall was spent getting acclimated to the hospice and caring exclusively for terminally-ill patients. The medical director was very helpful in teaching me about symptom control. While I brought a good bit of counseling experience to the work, I had not cared for many people with advanced cancer. The medications used to control the symptoms of advanced cancer are often very different than those used in general family practice. I devoted my time to becoming as good at symptom control as quickly as I could.

As I settled into the hospice work, my interest in NDEs began to intensify again. I attended the First Annual International Association of Near Death Studies in Georgetown, Maryland, in August of 1990. It was my first time in such a large group of people who had had NDEs and my first time sitting with a group of people who had undergone childhood NDEs. Words tumbled over words as we talked about how different we had felt from the other children, particularly with regard to sensitivity to violence and lack of interest in material possessions.

In the course of one interesting lunch there, someone mentioned having had unusual feelings in his head and spine since the NDE. As we discussed the phenomenon, we found that most of us had feelings of pressure or tingling in the top of our head and at the base of our spine from time to time. We didn't know what to make of it, but it was comforting to know that we were not alone. Many of us had not been troubled enough by the symptoms to go to a doctor; but those who did, did not come away with any explanation.

By the fall of 1990, I felt competent enough in hospice care to return to giving NDE talks. I had not been asked to give any talks over that summer. It was as if it were known that I was too overwhelmed with my new duties to be able to give talks also. But as soon as I felt ready, requests began coming in.

I gave my first talk that fall in my home for the hospice volunteers. Several people shared their own NDEs or those of their families or of patients they had known. As might be expected, the incidence of NDEs in hospice volunteers and other hospice workers is considerably higher than in the general population. A study that I did at the National Hospice Organization Annual Conference in 1992 showed that 15% of hospice workers have had NDEs.

That month I also spoke for the first time to a health careers class at a local high school. It was interesting to see how the usually diffused energy of young people focused as they listened to me talk about NDEs, hospice work, and how I became a physician. Several of them were even willing to share some of their own unusual experiences. It is often easier to share an unusual experience in a group of people that you don't know and will never see again than it is in a group of your peers. I was greatly impressed with their courage in telling their profoundly personal, moving stories to their peers. I was equally impressed with their peers for listening respectfully and often with empathy. Young people today seem to be much more mature and sensitive than most were thirty-five years ago when I was a teenager. I could not have imagined myself feeling safe talking about my NDE in a high school class. That first session began a series of annual talks that I gave to the health careers class. Each year I found it so uplifting to see that young people are becoming more and more attuned to understanding the importance of the mystical in their lives.

I finished the year with a formal slide presentation to the hospice employees. During the discussion period, employees shared stories that their patients had told them of events that occurred during the last few days of their lives. That opened the door for our discussing mystical events as a routine part of ongoing patient care conferences. Over time, we found that by honoring that part of our patients' realities with our attention we also honored ourselves and our work. It became a significant, uplifting part of team care conferences. The stories that I heard at these conferences added enormously to my understanding of NDEs, and forms the basis of much of my discussion in Part 2 of this book.

CHAPTER 4

Developing My Ideas about
NDEs and the Dying Process

⇥ LATE 1990 brought my first interview with a newspaper reporter —forty-five minutes by phone, as part of his preparation for an article that appeared in the local paper. Having heard all kinds of horror stories about being misquoted and misinterpreted, I was rather hesitant about the interview. But spreading the message about the significance of the life review in terms of the meaning of life was important enough to get me to agree to the interview. Before our conversation, I prayed and centered myself, asking to speak from my heart and not from my fear. On his part, the reporter listened carefully and then presented an article that I would have been pleased to have written myself.

The newspaper article presented my views to a whole different set of people than the talks had reached. Now anyone who read the editorial section of the *Houston Post* knew about my views. It gave an opening for many more people to approach me and share their experiences.

In February, 1991, I entered into a new phase of talking about NDEs. As part of my duties as a hospice physician, I began teaching a semi-annual class on "Living While Dying" to first-year medical students.

In the class dialogue, one student asked me how I kept from being depressed when working exclusively with dying patients. I reminded him that we are all going to die; hospice patients just know that their time is drawing nigh. Being so acutely aware of the fragility of life often results in their considering the importance of each moment, and being with people who are living life to the fullest in each moment is a great source of joy for me. That acute awareness of the importance of each moment is typical of people who have had NDEs, and it's one of the reasons that I am so comfortable with dying patients.

The main reason that I don't find the work depressing, however, is the incredible feeling of peace and oneness with God that I had during my own NDE. It was by far the most positive experience of my life. As a result, my honest belief as I care for dying patients is that I am caring for their bodies and keeping them comfortable while they prepare to go to that place where I have already been. Hence, though I have sadness for their families who will miss them, and sadness for them for the things that they won't have time to accomplish, I can help them complete what they can and know that they have a wonderful experience ahead of them. In fact, many of these people do have promising glimpses during the last few days of their lives.

That evening it seemed impossible to explain the fulfillment that I feel in working with terminally-ill patients without also talking about NDEs. So I did just that, although it was certainly not on my agenda when I entered the room.

As I shared my own NDE, everyone was silent in rapt attention. After I explained why I enjoy working with dying patients, I also mentioned the many stories that people have told me of being aware of their own cardiopulmonary resuscitations. They report not only seeing every detail of the resuscitation, but also being aware of what the doctors and nurses were *thinking* at the time.

In response to the students' anxious questions, I assured them that patients want respect and concern from them, not total knowledge. Their initial fear was that someone would "catch" them being afraid in their minds and not being sure what to do. I reminded them that in any cardiopulmonary situation, they would have more experienced people present until they became quite experienced themselves. Hence, they wouldn't be in control of the situation and the patient would not be harmed by their ignorance. They are supposed to be in a learning situation. However, it is important for them to be totally focused on the situation. I asked them always to remember that as the patient might be aware of their thoughts, it is important not to be critical of the patient or to let their mind wander to totally extraneous things during the resuscitation process.

First-year medical students are the best "physicians" to talk to about NDEs because they are generally open-minded. I hope that as a result of our conversation that night, those students will be sensitive to the possibility that patients might have an NDE during a close brush with death, and that they will be open to hearing about it and reassuring their patients.

As I reflected on the discussion on my way home that night, I remembered Dr. Michael Sabom's study in Atlanta, Georgia.[3] When Dr. Sabom read Raymond Moody's book, *Life after Life*, he was interested in the stories about NDEs, but wondered why no one had ever shared one with him since he was a cardiologist who frequently performed cardiopulmonary resuscitations.[4] When he did a study in the emergency room, he found that 43% of people told him about NDEs if they were interviewed in a sensitive way within a few days of their successful resuscitation. His study confirmed my hunch that people are not willing to share their experiences with their physicians unless the physicians are willing to listen. That was my message to those medical students that night. By the looks on their faces, I felt that it was a message that they would long remember.

⊰∦ ∦⊱

IN the spring of 1991, I spoke to the "Death and Dying" class at a Christian university. Because of the strong Christian influence in the university, I wondered how my talk would be received. Studies have shown that NDEs occur in 35–43% of people with cardiopulmonary resuscitations without regard to sex, age, culture, or religious beliefs.[5] Though clearly documented, this fact is very difficult for some people of strong religious persuasions to accept. I said it gently and tactfully, but I did say it.

In the question-and-answer time, someone asked if having an NDE made people more religious. I shared that it generally makes them more *spiritual,* but not necessarily more *religious.* (In my differentiation between the two words, I consider spirituality to be one's sense of connection with the Divine. I think of religion as the codified version of spirituality. Organized religion is not necessary for a profound sense of spirituality.) People shared their own experiences as well and the evening was as positive as the others had been. These talks were melting my own prejudices one by one about what people were willing to hear.

In the fall, a new challenge presented itself. I was asked to speak about NDEs to a monthly meeting of Muslims, Jews, and Christians—a group of people interested in exploring the differences and similarities among different cultures and religions. A good friend was a member of the group and thought that NDEs would be an interesting topic for their discussion. Since I knew very little about the various religious interpretations of NDEs, I thought that it would be a great opportunity for me to get some theologic perspective from the world's great religions. So, I planned to talk for twenty minutes and then listen for thirty minutes.

As it happened, a huge group attended the meeting, partly because the meeting had been advertised in the newspaper. The room was filled, and people stood in the hall and anteroom to hear the talk and discussion. To everyone's surprise, theological issues didn't even arise. As I completed telling my story and relaying some of the studies that have been done, the discussion period veered toward people's discussions of their own experiences. They spoke from their hearts about deeply moving experiences. There was a hush over the crowded room as we discussed the mysteries of the experience together. Suddenly, we were no longer Jews or Muslims or Christians, but human beings standing in awe of the mystery of God.

I heard later that discussions among the men in the group were often heated and divisive; but that day, we were all one. That day helped me to further understand the power of the NDE to bring us all together.

⊰⊱ ⊰⊱

I accepted another challenge in the spring of 1992. I was asked to do an afternoon workshop for family practice residents on "Death and Dying." In preparing for the workshop, it occurred to me that I didn't want to give them a lecture on the stages of acceptance of impending death. Most of them had heard a lecture on that in medical school.

When those stages were discovered in the 1960s, Elisabeth Kubler-Ross, was considered strange by her colleagues because she liked to talk to dying patients. She was learning from them how physicians could be more helpful. One result of that work was identifying what she called "five stages of dying": (1) denial and isolation, (2) anger, (3) bargaining, (4) depression, and (5) acceptance.[6]

Kubler-Ross herself was adamant that people don't move linearly through the stages in an organized fashion; the "stages" simply provide a framework to help delineate how a person is moving through a continuum. As medicine tends to do with so many things, however, the stages had been concretized—to such an extent that everyone had simply memorized them and felt no need to discuss them further.

I wanted to take the workshop beyond mere intellectual information and make it more experiential. An exercise I had done myself the year before at a workshop on dying put on by the Da Free John community seemed appropriate to try. In that exercise, we were asked to write down the answers to four questions during a period of silence. The four questions were: "What was your first experience with death?" "What were you told about death?" "What did you come to believe about death?" and "If you were dying, who would you want with you at the time?" The experience was meaningful to me when I did it, and I thought it would be helpful to the family practice residents in many ways.

The years of doing these exercises with medical students and residents have brought several discoveries. For example, although this first group of twelve people had been working intensely together for almost a year, they had related at a very superficial, intellectual level most of the time. Being more revealing to each other, particularly about emotions and feelings which were usually firmly suppressed, felt good to them. They found that their colleagues had the same fears and insecurities; it felt affirming to see that they were not as unusual as they feared they might be. Also, they discovered that they had very different levels of experience with regard to death. Some of them had only had a distant relative die, while others had experienced the death of a sibling or parent. Their views toward death were also dissimilar. Some believed strongly in an afterlife, while others were equally certain that when the body is dead, so is everything connected to that person except other people's memories of them. They also differed about whom they would want with them when they died. Some people wanted their whole families, others wanted a close friend or spouse, while others preferred to be alone.

We were all struck by the variety of answers in this relatively homogeneous group of young physicians. Recognizing such variety is very important if one is to be a good family physician who cares for dying patients and their families: *We must not assume anything about a person's beliefs, history, or preferred circumstances at the time of death.* A good family physician sits down with the patient and his or her family and learns to be helpful *in these particular circumstances.* Knowing the stages of acceptance of death is important, but it is not nearly enough.

I also spent some time explaining to this group what hospice does and why it is helpful to dying patients and their families. Hospice is a relatively new concept in the United States, and many lay people and physicians still don't understand what a hospice does. Hospice is a team concept of caring for a person who is terminally ill. By definition, a hospice patient must have received all of the active treatment that is possible or that he or she has deemed is appropriate. For example, patients with advanced cancer will have already received all of the chemotherapy, radiotherapy, and/or surgery that they and the doctors have deemed appropriate. When it is clear that such treatment is no longer desirable, hospice care may be requested.

The hospice physician provides symptom management while a nurse visits the patient's home to make sure that he or she is comfortable. A nurse's aide may help with baths, if so desired. A social worker helps the patient and the family prepare for the impending death, both psychologically and in terms of practical business matters. A chaplain is available for discussion of spiritual matters and to help prepare for the funeral at the appropriate time. Volunteers provide much-needed relief to the families who are providing twenty-four-hour care for their dying loved one. An in-patient unit is also available for back-up if the patient is having symptoms that are difficult to control at home, if the patient or the family doesn't want the death to take place at home, or if the family needs an extended break from caretaking.

After explaining the concept of hospice to the residents, I then told some hospice stories to get down to particulars and let them see how each individual member of the team is so important in the total care of the patient and family. Physicians are so frequently taught that they are "the captain of the ship" that they forget how important everyone else is to the running of the ship. It is so essential to inculcate beliefs in teamwork in physicians-in-training before they adopt bad habits and forget that they are a part of the healthcare *team*.

In the course of such student/physician workshops, I also talked about my NDE—it is impossible to discuss my beliefs about dying without expressing the profound influence that experience has had on my life. I also felt it crucial that I do the exercise with them, because the whole theme of the workshop was to show that while each of us may have different experiences and views, we are each a part of humanity as a whole.

⊰⊱

IN keeping with my goal of helping to make NDEs a commonly understood phenomenon that people feel comfortable discussing, I volunteered to give a workshop on NDEs at a statewide hospice meeting. In the discussion period after the talk, several people shared NDE stories about themselves or their patients.

Though this clearly was not a new topic to them, several of them said that they had never felt comfortable discussing these experiences in the team-care conferences at their hospice. I emphasized how important that sharing is in our hospice, since an NDE is often instrumental in moving the patient and family toward a greater acceptance of the impending death. It is also a sign that death is coming closer.

We all agreed that it is not at all unusual for patients to "see" dead relatives in the last few days of life. In fact, we even agreed that such visions are so common that they are one of the ways we know that the last few days of life are approaching. Nonetheless, most of the people had not been sharing that information with other members of their team when they learned of it. My experience has been that patients don't generally share the experience with each team member, but only with someone with whom they feel unusually close.

A profoundly moving part of that afternoon meeting came when an elderly woman spoke up to share her own NDE as a child. Listening to my story had evoked feelings of camaraderie in her strong enough to overcome the loneliness she also felt from having never talked about it before. With my arm around her, I held the microphone for her as she tremulously told the story of seeing the "upside-down funnel" and the Light during an episode of diphtheria as a young child. She shared how important it had been in her life, and how she had felt too uncomfortable to talk about it because of her fear that people would think she was crazy. The audience was moved to tears with her sincerity and emotion.

Someone who went to the conference the next year told me that this woman said that telling her story was a real watershed experience in her life. It had allowed her to feel more freedom to express who she really is. That experience and others like it are part of why I do my talks for whomever requests them.

❦

BY the fall of 1992 my NDE activities began to intensify. I had, of course, been meeting monthly with the "Exploring the Near-Death Experience" group, but had only given one talk all summer. In September, I met with the high school students in the health careers class. The teacher had moved to another school, so I taught her students at the new school. I was again struck with the openness of today's young people to talk about feelings and unusual experiences in front of each other. I felt so grateful for being alive at this time when the whole world is beginning to wake up to the realities that have always been here, but which we, for the most part, have refused to see. I was to remember this moment many times as I plunged into new, intense activities over the next several months.

I have noticed an ebb and flow to the rhythm of activities in my life. It seems as though I will have a period of relative private time followed by a period of accelerated activity. That has been particularly evident with my NDE activities since my original decision neither to seek them out nor to refuse offered activities. My own will has had little to do with my NDE activities. For the last several years, each day has started with a meditation and a centering on the activities of the day, aspiring to be attuned to divine guidance so that I may play my part well in the tapestry of life.

October, 1992 brought a call from a local television producer. The station had planned to interview a nationally-known person about NDEs the following morning, but he had canceled at the last minute. Would I talk with them live along with a few other local people who had had NDEs? I had never been on live television before, but agreed to the adventure before I had time to get too nervous.

They interviewed three of us at a time in two groups, and I was struck with how little time the format allowed to explain anything. Each segment lasted around three minutes before it was time for the next commercial. In the segment, each of us had around one minute to speak.

Then I remembered a friend (who had been on television frequently) saying that he always had one message he made sure was stated—no matter what questions the interviewer posed to him. So I made sure to say that the main messages of the near-death experience are that the purpose of life is to learn how to be loving to each other and that each moment really does matter.

I had never been backstage at a television show before, but did some observing before and after my time on stage. Everything was so frantic and rushed! A thirty-minute program touched on four different topics and had six commercials!

Life is so often lived in such a rush in modern-day America. Is it any wonder that many people have no idea of what their inner guidance might be? Listening to inner guidance requires time and inner stillness, things that many of us do not give ourselves.

Since that morning's glimpse into frantic living personified to the point of caricature, I have recalled that first television experience when I find myself beginning to lose my center. I know that no matter how busy I am, it is essential that I give myself whatever time is required to stay centered and in touch with my inner self. If I lose that, I have lost the most important part of myself. And unless it is a top priority, it won't get attended to at all.

The next experience came at my workshop at the National Hospice Organization Annual Meeting and Symposium in Nashville, Tennessee, later in October. With some some one hundred attendees at the workshop, the room was very crowded. Set up in typical lecture fashion, it was not designed for intimacy! Nonetheless, as one after another of the attendees told about NDEs that their patients had shared, a sense of wonder and acceptance arose among these fellow hospice workers.

I remember well one question that was asked at that workshop. This person knew someone who had become an alcoholic after his NDE. We talked for a few minutes about how difficult it is to adjust to the violence and unkindnesses practiced in this world after you have seen the way it was meant to be. I was reminded of the many talks that we had had in the NDE group in Houston about how difficult it is to adjust to the "real" world after an NDE. As I saw the softening in her face, I suggested that she might want to tell this man about the workshop and see if he would be interested in attending an NDE support group in his city, if there was one.

Shortly after, I did another workshop with the family practice residents on "Death and Dying." I used the same format as for the one in the spring, but this was, of course, a new group of people. This group happened to have had a lot more personal experiences with meaningful deaths than the previous group of young physicians had. They were much more willing to talk about feelings, presumably as a result of their own experiences. It became clear to me that young physicians have a need to talk about their first experiences with death as a doctor, so I began to incorporate that aspect of dealing with death in my workshops. I added a new question: "What was your first experience with death since starting medical school?" Over time I have found that physicians-in-training often will answer that question literally, but then go on to say that although that was their first experience, the one that really stuck in their mind was an entirely different one. Through such discussions of deeply significant events, we can connect at a deep level about the doctor/patient relationship and begin to discuss what we have learned from our patients.

⊰⊹⊱

BY the fall of 1992, I began to feel as though I were doing so many things that I was beginning to lose my feeling of centeredness. While I enjoyed each of the parts of my life, I knew that I was becoming overwhelmed and that a change was in order.

Reflecting on my professional life, I asked myself what I would like my job description to look like in a "perfect" world. Over the years, I have discovered the method that has worked best for me is to first notice my dis-ease in any situation. I then try to determine where I think that dis-ease is coming from—that is, what aspects of my current situation are contributing to the disharmony that I am feeling? With that background, I then ask myself how the situation could be changed to create ease without regard to anything other than my own wishes. When I am clear on that, I see how much can be accomplished with necessary modifications so that everyone involved is treated with respect in a cooperative manner. I don't expect to get everything I want, but I find that it is important to know what I prefer. I spent many years having much less than was possible because either

I didn't take the time to discover what I wanted or, if I knew what I wanted, I refused to risk rejection by asking for it.

In this situation, I knew that I was feeling too busy. I didn't have enough personal time to be in the stillness that feeds my soul. While I enjoyed every aspect of my life, some parts were more rewarding than others, and it was time to make some difficult decisions.

In addition to my professional activities, I was also a wife and mother, and I have always put those roles first: In the tapestry of life, we are the only ones who can weave our particular thread with our spouses and children. The threads of any other aspect of life can be picked up by someone else, but that thread is unique to the individual family and should be respected above all else. Over the years as I have observed other people, it has seemed a mark of being out of balance to be loved and respected at work and an unknown shadowy figure at home. I knew that with my intense schedule, I was in danger of becoming a shadow figure at home and that was entirely unacceptable to me.

Equally unacceptable was the feeling that I was getting out of touch with my inner guidance through too much activity. Hence, I spent some concentrated time in stillness listening for guidance about my career. After considerable meditation, I proposed a change in my job description. I asked to go to part-time work during which time I could work exclusively in the in-patient unit, leaving the home care and administrative work to the medical director, the other physician, and a new physician that they would need to hire in view of our expanding patient population. The proposal was accepted and a target date for the changes was established. I continued to do workshops and lectures throughout the winter as I looked forward to the altered schedule.

One workshop I co-presented with a professor of religion to a group of theologians. He was to present the theological aspects of the NDE; I was to talk about studies that had been done and my own experiences, both as a person who has had an NDE and as a person who has talked with many people who have had the experience. The conference was attended by ministers from all over the city of Houston as well as by several theology professors. I spoke first. Since I have essentially no background in theological studies, I was interested in hearing what the professor would say during his part of the talk, and steered clear of theologic comments during my own.

During the discussion period, one minister made an interesting comment. He said that NDEs are so common among parishioners and are becoming so well known among lay people that haven't had one that the Church is going to have to adapt itself to these new understandings. I hadn't been in a group of theologians before, but that comment is just the sort that I would like to hear from physicians. That people from all backgrounds and religious beliefs have very similar NDEs does indeed call for a major shift in the belief systems of many religions. Another difficult point for some theologians is that while one may be very uncomfortable during a life review as one experiences times of perpetrating unkindness on others, the Being of Light is there for support, not judgment. People who have NDEs become more loving people because they understand that the meaning of the world is to learn how to love well, not because they fear Hell.

I tried to convey to these clergymen the difficulties that people experience in adjustment after an NDE. In my conversations with people, many have spoken of having asked for help from their clergymen, only to be turned away—or to have their experience dismissed as a hallucination when it felt profoundly spiritual to them and had a great impact on their lives. People should be able to receive assistance with this from their ministers even more than from their doctors, since the experience is primarily a spiritual one that occurs during a particular physiologic phenomenon.

⋙ ⋘

TO my surprise, a major cancer center asked me to give a morning conference on NDEs to their pain service personnel in April, 1993. This center is one of the most famous cancer centers in the world with the most advanced techniques for treating cancer, including many experimental protocols for patients whose cancer is unresponsive to conventional treatments. In spite of their advanced techniques, many of their patients die of the cancer; terminally-ill patients were generally referred to our hospice.

I had not thought of the staff of this technically advanced hospital as being receptive to discussing NDEs, but that was a misconception on my part. The room was entirely filled for our early morning conference. Several people not actually on the pain service staff had heard about the conference and asked permission to attend. Along with physicians we had nurses, therapists, and a few administrative people who were particularly interested.

I gave my usual slide presentation describing the various aspects of the NDE, presented the research that had been done, talked about changes in people as a result of NDEs, and spoke about how professionals can help them adapt to those changes. I also talked about how common it was for our hospice patients to "see" dead relatives in the last few days of life. In the discussion period that followed, there was a remarkable lack of skepticism and essentially no antagonism (something that I had feared in such an intellectual setting.) In fact, several people volunteered NDEs that patients had shared with them over the years. They had come for the same reasons that people usually come to my talks. They had heard of these experiences or had one themselves and wanted a place to talk about it openly.

Several of the employees had had NDEs themselves, which seems natural when I think about it. People with NDEs frequently go into helping professions. Caring for people with cancer who are sick with the treatments and with the disease itself seems a natural thing for a person who has had an NDE to do.

The atmosphere in the room at one of the highest institutions of learning in the country was no different than when I spoke at any other group. It seemed to me that the world was really changing with regard to its acceptance of alternate realities.

CHAPTER 5

Deepening the Process

◈ IN June, 1993, I reported some of my findings at the annual meeting of the International Association of Near-Death Studies (IANDS) in St. Louis, Missouri. At the National Hospice Organization Annual Meeting in October, 1992, I had asked the workshop participants to complete a questionnaire exploring their knowledge of NDEs. Seventy-five people had completed the questionnaire. The IANDS talk was based on the findings from that survey and on my own experience at our hospice.

In my October survey, 75% of the participants had had someone tell them about an NDE. The number of people who had heard them from hospice patients and those who had heard them from friends or family was about equal. I felt that this high percentage might be due to the fact that hospice workers are generally nonjudgmental people who are good listeners. The ones I polled also had chosen to attend my workshop while five other different workshops were also going on, so clearly my group was more interested in NDEs than the average hospice worker.

Another interesting statistic was that 15% of the people who took my survey had undergone an NDE. Since the average in the population at large is 5% (based on a 1982 Gallup poll), it is reasonable to surmise that people who have had NDEs tend to gravitate toward hospice work. That is no surprise, really, since people who have had an NDE are generally no longer afraid of dying. As one of the important tasks of hospice work is to help people and their families prepare for death, a background in NDEs is very helpful to hospice workers.

Several people in the audience in St. Louis were either hospice workers or people who had lost a close family member. They talked about how helpful it was to have the knowledge of NDEs when they worked through their acceptance of the deaths. Knowledge about NDEs doesn't keep a person from missing his or her loved one, but it does help to alleviate anxieties about the after life.

At that same conference, there were a couple of talks about the influence of NDEs on the *kundalini* experience. The *kundalini* experience has been described as a rising of energy from the base of the spine, through the spine, and into the head. Through the ages, it has been consciously sought by Eastern meditators as a realignment of energies that leads to enlightenment when complete. Through the years, spontaneous accounts of movement of *kundalini* energy have been described as well. The latter are frequently quite disruptive to the individuals involved, because they were totally unprepared for the experience and didn't know what to make of the changes that they were feeling in their bodies. The speakers mentioned that changes of *kundalini* energy are not uncommon in people who have had NDEs.

All this information reminded me of my discussion two years previously at the IANDS conference in which several people who had undergone NDEs talked about strange feelings and tingling in the crown of their heads. I wondered if those feelings might be associated with the *kundalini* energy. It will be very interesting to see if research in coming years does bring these experiences together.

⇥ ⇤

WHEN I began working exclusively in the in-patient hospice unit, I felt that a rebirth had occurred for me. It was so wonderful to have all the time that I wanted to be with dying patients and their families.

I structured the job description so that I would care for anyone who came into the in-patient unit. I was on call during the week and on one weekend per month. On the weekend call, I was on call for the entire hospice; but during the week, I was on call for just the in-patient unit. I would frequently go into the unit two or three times per day depending on admissions, which was easy because I lived only a mile and a half away.

With the part-time work, I felt my life coming back into alignment. I was able to reach a much deeper level of stillness in meditation and was able to hear my inner guidance again quite clearly. It was much easier to stay in the present moment rather than to have my mind wander off to something that just happened or was about to happen. It was also wonderful to really "be" with my family again.

With the opportunity to be with the dying patients and their families on a daily basis, I was able to be much more helpful to them in their last days and to learn much more about NDEs and the dying experience. Another bonus of the new schedule was that the in-patient team was now a more cohesive unit since there was only one doctor rather than a rotating group of doctors. Through our weekly team conferences and daily discussions, we were able to work together to help the patients and their families with more continuity than ever before. It was a most rewarding time for all of us who were involved in that setting.

Throughout the year, I continued to give talks to a variety of groups. Several social workers at one of them relayed incidents where patients had told their physicians about their NDEs and had received negative responses. Either the physicians had dismissed the experiences as dreams or, worse, had consulted psychiatrists who were uninformed about NDEs and in their ignorance tried to treat the experience with medications. I was reminded of how much work still needs to be done to educate physicians about NDEs.

An experience with medical students that same month offered a promising contrast. During a class on attitudes toward dying and hospice work, we initially discussed our own attitudes toward death and dying. As always when I talk about my attitudes toward dying, I had to mention my own NDE. They were very interested in hearing about it, so I told my story and then several of the group of some twenty-five young people told of NDEs that had been told to them by friends or relatives. It brought great hope that this new generation of physicians in training will be more supportive of NDEs and other unusual experiences than their colleagues have been. I encouraged them to keep their sense of wonder as they go through the training process, and reminded them that everything that will be known is not yet known. What they will learn in medical school is the current "truth" as the medical profession understands it now. That "truth" may well change in their lifetimes, which is an important fact to keep in mind as the information is being learned.

Another moving and hopeful experience occurred that year one evening with a large group of high school students, just before their spring break. Although they had been in very rowdy spirits before we began our discussion, they quieted down immediately, really listened, and focused on the stories. After I had shared with them some of the hospice and NDE stories, they began sharing their own experiences. They were attentive to each other and very supportive. I was again very encouraged about the directions that our world is taking.

Reflecting on the seven years since I had first begun to focus consciously on the deeper experiences of life, I realized how much more connected I felt with that little girl who had been so changed by the NDE. In the least conscious parts of my mind, I had always been connected with the deeper realities, but I had allowed the details of my life to interfere with my inner knowing. My involvement with NDEs and the hospice work as well as the regular meditation had allowed me to integrate all of the aspects of my being.

With reference to the analogy presented in the prologue, I felt that I had stopped living in the ante-chamber exclusively and could now freely move between the ante-chamber and the drawing room. The balance felt really good. I wanted to share what I had learned, and, thus, this book was created.

⇥ PART 2 will discuss what I have learned about NDEs, death, and dying in these past several years. Many questions remain, and these will only be answered as we begin to feel free to share our experience of alternate realities with each other. As we feel free to talk about both positive and negative experiences, we will all benefit from the exchange.

PART 2

What I've Learned about NDEs and the Dying Process

❧ ❦

CHAPTER 6

How NDEs in Terminally-Ill Patients Appear to Differ from Those in Acute Events

⊰ FROM talking with people who have had NDEs in all kinds of situations, I've come to some conclusions as to how NDEs in terminally-ill patients differ from those that occur in acute situations. First, the episodes in terminally-ill patients do not necessarily come at times of severe physiologic compromise as they do in people with acute NDEs. Second, seeing dead relatives is much more common in terminally-ill patients than in people with acute NDEs. Third, a life review is more common in acute NDEs than in NDEs of hospice patients. Fourth, the purpose of the NDE in acute situations appears to be to help the person learn to live in more loving ways, whereas the purpose of an NDE in terminally-ill people seems to be to help them die in peace. Several stories will illustrate these points.

First, it is extremely common for terminally-ill patients to have an NDE in the last few days of life, and it may not necessarily occur at a time of severe physiologic compromise. On several occasions, I have entered the room of a patient who was clearly conversing with someone that I was not seeing. If a family member was in the room, it was usually reported that this had been going on for some time. Unlike a patient who is having hallucinations, these patients will answer my question coherently and then return to what they were doing before I entered the room if I interrupt them. They are having an important communication at that time. In fact, it is not unusual for them to share that communication with me and/or their relatives either a few hours later or the next day.

These conversations have usually taken place with a deceased relative. But some people have told me that they were talking with a religious figure, usually Jesus, or even with a completely unknown figure (although that is much less common). My experience is that many more terminally-ill patients visit with deceased relatives than do people who have an NDE under acute conditions. Generally speaking, it is extremely helpful to the dying person to communicate with these deceased relatives.

One elderly man whose wife had died of Alzheimer's disease two years before he contracted terminal cancer was delighted when he "visited" with her in her pre-Alzheimer state. He exclaimed that he had "got my wife back!" They had been wonderful companions to each other for some fifty years before the Alzheimer's disease took her away from him long before her death. He had cared for her himself for the last several years of her life, and it was very painful for him to see the person that he knew slip away while her body remained.

After the "visitation" experience, he believed that he would be reunited with his beloved wife in her pre-Alzheimer condition. That belief allowed him to approach the last few days of his life with equanimity, and even a measure of joy.

⊸ AN encounter with Jesus made all the difference to another hospice patient. She was a very angry woman in her forties who was absolutely devoted to her family of several children, most of whom were still at home when she contracted cancer. As her body began to be overcome by the cancer, she steadfastly refused to talk about her terminal illness to anyone, including her husband. She vehemently insisted that she was too young to die and that it simply wasn't going to happen. She was not finished yet and she didn't want to talk further about it.

Her pain was difficult to manage because emotional pain and anger intensify the physical pain of terminal cancer. In spite of multiple medication adjustments and multiple visits from the social worker and the chaplain, some pain remained, in large part due to her distressing emotional condition. When I prayed about ways to assist her in her pain, I got the clear feeling that she would be helped, but not in the usual ways that our patients were helped. Two days later, she had a profound mystical experience that completely changed her attitudes toward life and her impending death.

In her mystical experience, she found herself in a beautiful meadow with her mother, who looked young and healthy though she had died several years before. She assured her that she would be with her and that she would be in a calm and peaceful place. She found herself relaxing and re-experiencing the love that she had felt for her mother. As she turned to the side, she saw Jesus with his arms outstretched and a loving expression on his face. The woman felt a strong pull toward Jesus. However, she remembered her family at home and realized that she had not yet told them "goodbye." She told Jesus that she was not yet ready to come, but that she would soon be ready. With that declaration, she found herself back in her body in her bed at home.

Over the next two days, one by one the children were called in privately to her bedroom where she told them how much she loved them and that she would be watching over them in her death in just the way that she had in her life. She spent time with her husband, helping him to prepare for her death and single parenting. When she had done what she could to prepare them, she said that she was ready to go. Within a few hours she became unresponsive and then died peacefully the next day. The grieving process was much easier for her family because of her experience than it would have been had she died in confusion and anger, denying her imminent death.

⊰ NDEs in terminally-ill patients do seem to have the purpose of helping them to prepare for death. Although people often find it very useful to spend a great deal of time in the last weeks and months of life contemplating their lives and trying to make peace in areas where forgiveness is needed, they rarely tell me about life reviews in their NDEs. In contrast, life reviews are fairly common in people with acute NDEs.

One person with an acute NDE, for example, told me that he "saw" every event that had occurred in his life, including the times that he was extremely unkind. The feeling he drew from the Being of Light who watched his life review with him was that it was all perfect, even the "mistakes." It was all part of the lessons that he came here to learn. Because of this life review, he revised his understanding of the meaning of life. Prior to the experience, he had seen life as a series of random events that occur until death ends it all. Because of the experience, he realized that life has meaning and that it is important to learn to be loving. Furthermore, the experience convinced him that there is more to life than just this life on Earth. As a result of the experience, he believes that the spirit goes on beyond this life.

A similar change in perspective occurred in a hospice patient, although she didn't have a life review. This lady was an atheist and extremely angry about dying young, when she had barely begun to live. Her husband held similar views. As the patient became less and less responsive, her husband sat by her side in intense anger and grief.

When the patient had been unresponsive for two days, she suddenly awakened to tell her husband of a remarkable experience. She had found herself going down a tunnel that was at first frightening because of the sense of lack of control and the speed of the traveling. However, she began to be attracted to a bright light at the end of the tunnel. To her amazement, as she approached the light, she felt surrounded by an incredible feeling of peace and love and she saw Jesus with his arms outstretched. Her tension, anger, and pain melted away. She felt that she had a choice about staying, but she wanted to tell her husband about the experience since it was so helpful and so different than what they had both believed about death. With the decision made, she found herself back in her body struggling toward consciousness to share her story.

After sharing this story, she became peacefully unresponsive and died a day or two later in peace. Needless to say, that shared experience was enormously helpful to her husband in the grieving process. Learning how to live life had not been so important to the hospice patient as learning how to die peacefully; perhaps that is why she didn't undergo a life review.

This story is also a profound example of intense personal love. It is extremely difficult to pull back from a deeply comatose state in terminal cancer; but, somehow, this young woman's love and concern were so strong and so deep that she was able to pull herself back enough to tell the story to her grieving husband.

⇥ Sometimes the encounters in NDEs of terminally-ill patients are more mysterious. One man who was quite clear-headed, for example, kept seeing a small child in the room during the last couple of weeks of his life. As far as he could remember, this was no one that he knew. They never said anything to each other. The child was simply silently present: He would sit or stand and not move about at all, and he had a peaceful energy about him. The man told his wife about the child because it was so puzzling. We never did understand the significance of the silent witness. In addition to the strange child in the corner of the room, this same man frequently "saw" dead relatives throughout the last several days of his life. In fact, his wife said that he seemed to be in that world more often than he was in this one those last several days. I've often wondered if he discovered the identity of that mysterious child after his death.

⇥ Most terminally-ill patients who have NDEs encounter dead relatives. In contrast, visits with dead relatives occur only occasionally in acute NDEs. One young woman shared with me an NDE that occurred to her during surgery that went awry. She met a soldier who introduced himself as her grandfather, Samuel. She had never met her grandfather, as he had died in his forties before she was born. Her "visiting" grandfather said that he wanted to tell her how sorry he was that he had been unable to demonstrate love to his son (her father) and that he understood that that was why his son was unable to demonstrate love to her. He went on to say that if there was one thing that he could have changed about his life, that would have been the thing.

When she recovered from the anesthesia, she asked her father about her grandfather. In all her years, he had never even mentioned his father's name to her before. He said that his name was Samuel, and that he didn't want to talk about him. Later, in a drawer, she found a picture of a young soldier who looked just like the Grandfather Samuel that she met in her NDE.

She said that the experience was extremely helpful to her in learning to be understanding toward her own father's difficulty expressing affection. She credited that experience with helping her get through her teen years with this very controlling father. Even though her experience was with a dead relative, its purpose was clearly to help her live her life with more understanding, not prepare for her death.

A similar experience occurred to a young woman during a cardiac arrest that occurred during surgery. As she watched her resuscitation from the corner of the operating room, she was amazed to see a teenaged girl, dressed in old-fashioned clothes, in the other corner of the room; the girl was dressed in a gingham dress with a straw bonnet over red hair, quietly watching the resuscitation. The patient was puzzled by the presence of that young girl in the operating room, but didn't think too much about it until several months later when visiting her grandmother's house. On a whim, they decided to clean out the attic. As she went through an old chest, she happened upon a photo of just that same figure. She had never been in the attic before and felt certain that she had never seen that picture before.

When she asked her grandmother about the girl in the photo, she was told that it was a photo of her mother at the age of eighteen. The mother had died when this woman was still an infant, and she had no conscious recollection of what her mother had looked like. Suddenly, the operating room experience made a whole lot more sense to her. As she told the story, I had a sense that her mother had been silently watching over her to be her guide in case the resuscitative attempt was not successful.

◈ In some ways, NDEs in terminally-ill patients bridge the gap between mystical experiences that occur in people who are not ill at all and acute NDEs that occur during cardiac arrests or auto accidents. In general, mystical experiences in people who are not ill tend to occur because of a deep yearning for understanding. Occasionally, they occur "out-of-the-blue," but often they are as a result of a deep longing. Likewise, people who have NDEs in the terminal phase of their lives are often not physiologically compromised at that moment, but available for an intense mystical experience because of the uncertainty that they are feeling.

I believe that we inhibit our ability to live with the mystical by being so involved in daily activities that we never look up. An acute NDE occurs in a situation that absolutely grabs our attention, no matter what we were doing or thinking the moment before the event. For the terminally-ill person, there is a sense of pulling away from the daily activities and looking ahead to death and beyond. Thus, they may be more available to mystical experiences. Similarly, the person with deep longing is available to the experience.

Several stories of people having the experience of going down a tunnel and being in the presence of God during a particularly intense sexual orgasmic encounter support this hypothesis. These people happened to be men. My thought is that they were able to let go of the details of daily life long enough to be available to the mystical. Of interest, the NDE created the same changes in their lives and values as NDEs that occur during acute physiologic events.

Furthermore, mystical experiences are not uncommon in people who are meditating in order to control hypertension. Herbert Benson, for example, was quite surprised to find his patients having mystical encounters with God when they meditated on a single word or phrase.[7] His work at Harvard Medical School was exclusively designed to elicit the relaxation response in order to help people with hypertension and chronic stress: There was no emphasis on the spiritual in the program as he designed it, but people often talked about having spiritual experiences. My understanding of that phenomenon is that

God will enter our field of awareness any time we hold still enough in body and mind to notice His presence.

With regard to a deep longing for the spiritual, one man told of a time of deep despair in his life. Nothing seemed to be working for him. Several close relatives had died in the past two years, he had been laid off because of company cuts in a poor economic environment, and his wife had left him. Lying on the couch, contemplating his condition and considering suicide, he sincerely asked, "What is the meaning of life?" Immediately he found himself in a mystical experience in which he actually felt the presence of God and felt the love that we ourselves are meant to be. In that moment, he understood that we are not about the details of life, but we are about learning to love in each moment. After that experience, he was able to experience life in a new way and to look for opportunities to be loving. Thoughts of suicide became a thing of the past.

⇨ Observing the peaceful death or NDE of a loved one can be extremely helpful in the grieving process. Several mothers have told me of these experiences.

One mother told the story of her three-year-old daughter who lay dying in her arms after a long illness. As she died, a beautiful peaceful look came over the child's face and she seemed to radiate light. The mother knew at that moment that her child was perfectly all right and protected. Although she missed her little girl, she did not grieve as much as people expected her to because she knew that she was at peace.

A little boy had cancer. By the time that he was terminally-ill with it at two years of age, he had spent more than half of his life in hospitals with chemotherapy and complications of the illness. He was a frail little boy who appeared wise beyond his years although he could say only a few words because of his young age. During the two days before his death, his mother and grandmother both witnessed him on at least two occasions having what seemed to be an NDE in his crib. When they watched him from the doorway of his bedroom (where he couldn't see them), they saw him stand up in the corner of his crib and lift his arms up to an unseen figure. At those times, he seemed to glow and had a beautiful smile on his face. No one was in the room except for the little boy and his "angel." He died peacefully a day later with a beautiful smile on his face. That radiant death was a real source of comfort to his family who had watched their tiny son suffer so much in his short life. They felt comforted to know that he was finally in a safe place and no longer in pain.

While these children were too young to talk about their experiences and their parents surmised what was happening from their actions, an older boy helped his family prepare for his death by sharing his experience with them. He was a teenager with cancer. A few days before his death, he had an NDE during which he felt himself in the presence of Jesus. After he shared his experience with his family, family members were able to let go of much of their anger and focus on saying "good-bye."

These experiences happen at all stages of life. One woman told of the profound changes that her husband underwent when he had an NDE one week before his death from cancer. He declared to her that he had "seen the face of God" while being surrounded by light. Although he had never been particularly religious, he now declared that he knew beyond a shadow of a doubt that there was a God and that he wanted to go right then. He insisted that all of the tubes (IV's, etc.) be removed, and then he relaxed. To his chagrin, he lived another week—not particularly in physical discomfort, but in impatience. His NDE spawned a deep interest in mysticism in his wife, a passion that she is still pursuing some twenty years after his death. In that way, his NDE made a very profound difference in her life.

The grieving process was also much easier for a middle-aged woman who was with her father when he died. Her mother had died several years earlier, and she was feeling very sad contemplating being without parents. Right before he died, her father smiled broadly and said, "I'm coming across the river, Honey. Wait for me!" Then he died. The grieving daughter remembered that smile on his face for the rest of her life.

◈ Because the dying process is gradual in terminally-ill patients, some aspects of it are more apparent than they are when acute illnesses or traumatic episodes lead to an acute NDE. Several hospice volunteers have shared with me their perceptions of what happens with people dying of terminal illness.

Volunteers are particularly aware of these aspects, for several reasons. First, they have the *time* to be aware. Unlike the staff who are busying themselves with the details of patient care, the volunteers' sole purpose is just to "be there." Second, they do not have the emotional load that the family has. The family is attentive to the dying patient, of course, but much of their attention is drawn to their own pain, uncertainty, and anger. Third, people drawn to hospice work are particularly sensitive and spiritual; they are likely to be aware of very real energy shifts that other people just don't notice because of lack of sensitivity.

One male volunteer shared the story of his first hospice patient. He visited a young man, who was dying of AIDS, in his home on several occasions during the last few months of his life. During those visits, he came to view him as a wonderful friend and teacher. As the patient came closer to death, he allowed the volunteer to share his internal processes as he gradually shifted from a physical being to an entirely spiritual one. In the final few days, they experienced times when the patient did not seem to have a physical body at all; his limbs felt as if "they were water." The volunteer felt as though he could pass his hands through the patient's arms in those times when he hovered between this plane and the next one. When he made his transition, the volunteer was there to hear the patient say, "It's beautiful!" as he died with a beatific smile. I feel that he was able to do that easy transition over the last few days because he had resolved his issues in this lifetime and was, therefore, able to focus on his transition process.

One volunteer likes to sit with people who are so near to death that they are unresponsive. If these people have no family members with them, she just sits with them as they make their transition. Her very calm, centered presence is a real blessing to these people as they die. In the stillness and calm, she has often felt their spirits leave before she has noticed that their breathing has stopped.

A young male volunteer told of being with a patient shortly after he died. While waiting for the patient's family to arrive, the volunteer was dozing on the window seat when he felt a breeze go by that raised the hairs on his arm. It felt to him that the spirit of the deceased person was blowing by.

One afternoon a very elderly man with endstage dementia was brought to the in-patient unit with a severe infection that had been unresponsive to antibiotics. As I examined him, it became clear that he was actively dying and we called in his family. While we waited for the family to arrive, a nurse and I sat with him. I gave him oxygen and medicine to help with his breathing. As I looked at his face, I recognized the all-too-common look of the person who is completely demented. At that stage of the dementia, people have a wild, frightened look in their eyes; my experience has been that they do not recognize anyone, but are frightened of everything as they have become prisoners of their own minds.

That afternoon was rather quiet for me, and I decided to stay with him until his family arrived or until he died, whichever occurred first. Standing next to him, I began breathing in synch with his breathing while thinking peaceful thoughts. There was no activity, just our quiet breathing together. Slowly, his breathing began to relax and I could tell that he was slipping away. I had been touching his shoulder gently to maintain human contact, but then I gently removed my hand and stepped away from the bed about six inches. After a few more breaths which became successively slower and shallower, he suddenly opened his eyes and looked fully into my eyes. It felt to me that there was real recognition and gratitude in his look. He took one more breath and died peacefully.

That was a very important learning experience for me. I had always assumed that someone that demented would not be able to have any more human contact in this lifetime. It really amazed me to be so sure that he had really seen me in that last breath. In that last moment, he was probably more alive than he had been in the last several years of his life. The nurse who had observed us during the last few minutes and I talked later about the experience. We had both felt blessed and privileged in the holy atmosphere of that experience.

Another profoundly moving experience that came from just not being too busy with details to notice the really important things was with a Korean Christian family as their father died. As the elderly gentleman lay dying peacefully in his bed, his extended family of twelve people circled his bed, held hands, and sang "Amazing Grace" in Korean. They invited me to join them. As I hummed along with their singing, he opened his eyes, smiled at each of them, and died with a smile on his lips and "Amazing Grace" in his ears. It was a truly holy moment for all of us. They completed the song in their circle in order to send him off in peace. They then hugged each other. I felt so blessed to have been there at that moment and to have been wise enough (for once) to stop what I was doing and fully participate in life and death.

Pausing to fully participate in life and death may well be the main message of hospice work and NDEs. We miss so much of what life is most about when we are so busy *doing* that we do not take time to *be.* When we are in a mode of *being,* we are open to subtle energies and profound experiences. When we are in a mode of rapid *doing,* we are closed to the profound moments of life unless we are slammed into an NDE by a car accident or a heart attack! Terminally-ill people who have NDEs are usually more in a mode of *being* and, hence, they frequently come and go between both worlds.

CHAPTER 7

Visitations From Dead Relatives

⊷ VISITATIONS from dead relatives are so common as to deserve a whole chapter of their own. While such visitations during NDEs were discussed in the previous chapter, these visitations occur under other circumstances as well. People are often "notified" of a death by the deceased person, for example. Visitations are also quite common in the days or first few weeks after the death of a close relative. Most of these visits seem to have the purpose of reassuring the grieving relatives or friends. Finally, a visitation from a dead relative sometimes brings a warning or comfort during difficult circumstances.

As mentioned before, visitations from dead relatives during the dying process are universally comforting to the person having the experience. One frightened young woman had a powerful experience with a cousin who had died as a child. In her experience, her elementary-aged deceased cousin took her by the hand as they wandered through sunlit woods along a path. He said that he had a wonderful surprise to show her. As they went down the path, the woods cleared and they saw a crystal-clear lake with porpoises swimming lazily about. The whole area was lit with a soft light. Her cousin whispered to her, "Pretty soon you'll be swimming with the porpoises." With that, the cousin dove into the water and began playing with the porpoises. When the young woman returned to her room, she told her family that she was no longer afraid of dying because pretty soon she would be swimming with the porpoises. Though she had some frightened moments, she remained peaceful, overall, for the last few days of her life as a result of the experience.

In my hospice experience, visitations from dead relatives are one of the ways that we know that a person is entering into the final days of life. Almost always when there is a visitation, the dead relative appears in perfect health at the prime of life. As might be imagined, this is especially comforting to couples who were married for many years before the spouse died. It is equally true for children who see their deceased grandparents or parents. (It is interesting to note that no one has told me about a visitation from someone who is still alive.)

One man's experience with deceased relatives was so exciting and joyful that he woke up his wife in the middle of the night to tell her about it. He was ready to go right then, but was disappointed to remain for several more days.

Sometimes the visits have an element of humor to them. One man returned from a coma and reported that his deceased father had told him to get the suitcase out from under his bed. Indeed, during his comatose state, family members had put an extra suitcase under his bed. There was no way that he could have seen that suitcase because he could no longer sit up in his debilitated state, and he certainly couldn't lean over far enough to look under the bed. Why his father told him to get the suitcase out from under the bed will forever remain a mystery!

⇥ PEOPLE frequently feel the moment of death of a loved one. Several people have talked about being awakened from a sound sleep with the positive knowledge that a particular loved one had died. Sometimes these deaths were expected and sometimes they were not. In a short time, they have received the phone calls that confirm the fact the persons died at the exact moment that they were awakened from their sleep. The following stories are several examples of people who have known of the death of a relative before they were told.

One interesting story was told by a nurse who had cared in a hospital for a terminally-ill adolescent for six months prior to the teenager's death. One night at 2:35 A.M., the nurse awoke at home from a sound sleep and felt that the boy was standing next to her bed. She could see him very clearly and was surprised to see that he was wearing a new baseball cap. She asked him what he was doing in her room. The boy said that he had come to tell her that he was all right and that the nurse should hug his mother for him when she saw her in three months. The nurse then went back to sleep, thinking that she must have had a very vivid dream. She couldn't shake the feeling the next morning, so she called the hospital to check on the boy. After a long pause, the other nurse told her that the boy had died unexpectedly at around 3 A.M.

The nurse had nearly forgotten the "dream" when she was attending a funeral of another patient three months later. The first patient's mother walked up to her at the cemetery—even though she had always sworn that if her son died, she would never return to that city. The nurse told her about her vision and asked if she had ever seen that baseball cap. The mother laughed and said that she had bought the hat for her son, but had not yet had time to take it to the hospital on the night that her son died. She said that she, too, had felt the presence of her son intermittently over the past three months. It was very comforting to her that her son had wanted to reassure her, but still puzzling as to how he knew about the baseball cap and how he knew that his mother would be in the city in three months and would meet the nurse at that time.

One woman talked about an agreement that she had made with her terminally-ill aunt. They had carried on many discussions about the possibility of an after-life, and her aunt had agreed to try to let her know what she was learning if she could do it without frightening her. A couple of days before her aunt died, she was awakened at 4:25 A.M. by a tingling feeling that ran through her entire body and a ringing sound in both ears. She could hear someone trying to tell her something, but was unable to catch the words because of the loud ringing. Finally, she realized that the voice was her aunt's. She wondered if her aunt had died at that moment, but she hadn't—she had just become comatose. When she visited the next morning, she found her aunt completely unresponsive whereas she had been able to squeeze her hand purposefully the night before. Her aunt died peacefully two days later, not having regained consciousness again prior to her death.

◈ A small boy died in a car accident in a distant city. At the time of his death, he "visited" his favorite cousin who lived on the opposite coast of the U.S. She had a vision of him standing before her perfectly happy and peaceful. He communicated to her that she should not be sad for him. It was enormously helpful to her to have had that contact with her favorite cousin. Shortly thereafter, the phone rang and she was officially notified of his death. She didn't grieve as much as people had expected that she would, because she knew that he was at peace.

◈ TWO hours before his mother called to say that his sister had died, a young man was awakened from a sound sleep by the unmistakable feeling of his sister's presence. She seemed to be at the foot of his bed as she told him that she had killed herself because she was in just too much pain. She assured him that there was nothing that he could have done to have prevented her death. She also said that she felt that she was in a better place than she had been while in her body. His vision was confirmed by his mother's conversation some two hours later. His sister had indeed killed herself the day before and her body had just been found. (It is interesting to note that most people who have had an NDE during a suicide attempt feel that suicide is not a viable way of dealing with problems. However, they generally do not have negative experiences. That is just something that they learn during their life reviews.)

◈ ANOTHER woman talked about her aunt's death. At the time of her death, the aunt had simultaneously appeared to several family members to let them know that she was fine. She had always been a strong-willed spiritual woman and no one in the family was surprised by her final act.

◈ BECAUSE a young woman listened to her intuition, she was able to be very helpful to her childhood friend in the final days of the friend's life. Although they had not seen each other in months, they had been good friends from the age of eight and had been very close. Although she had not thought of her friend in quite a while, she suddenly began thinking of her constantly and had the strong feeling that she was in danger.

After a couple of days of intense preoccupation with these intuitions, she attempted to call her in the distant city where she lived. When she didn't answer after several phone calls, she called her friend's landlord to check on her. When the landlord opened her friend's apartment at her insistence, he found that the young woman was close to death from a hemorrhaged brain tumor. She was taken to the hospital where she stayed for a week until her death. During that time, she was able to heal much that had occurred between herself, her family, and her estranged boyfriend. It was a very important time for her to complete her unfinished business.

❧ A woman told of being "notified" of a good friend's death who died some thousand miles away. At the same time that people were telling her that he was all right, she felt his presence and the clear certainty that he was dead. From talking with the hospital and looking at the records, she learned that he did indeed die at precisely the time that she felt his presence. The other people had been lying to her so that family members could be with her when she was told that he was dead.

❧ PEOPLE are not only "notified" of deaths, they are also frequently comforted by visitations for some time after the loved one has died.

One woman told the story of her husband's visitation the night after he had died. He was elderly and very debilitated at the time of his death from a long battle with cancer. The night after he died, she had the very strong impression that he was lying down in bed with her and holding her. In that experience, he was no longer the sick old man that she remembered, but the young man that she had married. She was very clear that this felt very different than a dream.

Over the next two years, she found it very difficult to begin her life as a single woman. She found herself constantly thinking of him and not really paying attention to this world or trying to form any relationships.

At the time that we talked, some two years after her husband's death, she had recently had a very disturbing vision. She had "seen" him in heaven looking happy and healthy with other companions. In this "dream," he seemed to know that she was there, but was not paying any attention to her. She felt sad for several days after the dream. I felt that she was being supported "from the other side" in the very appropriate direction of getting on with her life on Earth instead of merely waiting to join her deceased husband.

The story told by another widow supports that interpretation of her experience. This second widow felt her husband's presence frequently during the first few days after his death. He seemed to be hovering around to make sure that she was doing all right. Then she didn't sense his presence for several months, but did continue to mourn his loss. One afternoon several months after his death, he told her telepathically that it was time for her to complete her mourning and to get on with her life. He went on to say that he would not be back again as he was going on with his journey, as well. She was so shocked by what she had heard that she gave it a lot of thought and began to see the wisdom of what she had been told. She realized that she had been so involved with the grieving that she had not yet begun to re-fashion her own life. At her husband's request, she did begin to live her life as a single woman, not as a woman who was only half there because half of her had been taken away with his death.

⊰ ONE young widower was very comforted by a "visit" from his wife some four months after a car accident in which she was killed instantly at the young age of thirty-two. She came quite unexpectedly and assured him that she was in a good place and that they would see each other again some day. Since he had never been able to tell her "good-bye" because of the suddenness of her death, that visit was especially important to him. It also helped to be able to reassure their three small children that Mommy was all right.

IN any lecture that I have given, almost invariably someone will talk about reassurance from deceased relatives. The above are just a handful of examples from a large number of stories that I have been told. From all the stories, though, I can not tell why it is that some people come back to visit and some don't. The theme of the visits always seems to be reassurance; but there are many people who would love to be reassured who don't get a visit. Their circumstances certainly seem very similar to those who do get reassured, so I am not sure what the difference is. I do know, however, that it is reassuring for many of these people to hear other people's stories, even if they don't have a similar one themselves. From that perspective, I would encourage people who have their own stories of visitations from loved ones to share them with other people. That is one of the ways that we will expand our view of the world. To do that, we need to be open and honest with each other about these kinds of experiences.

Less common than "reassurance" visits, but, certainly very powerful, are visits from dead relatives that keep the living from harm. Several examples will illustrate this type of visitation.

One woman told of a visitation from her mother several years after her mother's death. She felt strongly that her mother was trying to warn her about some danger, but she couldn't understand what the warning was. She asked her mother to give her a sign about the danger and then went to bed. The next morning as she was reading the newspaper, a shock went through her as she glanced at an advertisement for annual preventive examinations. She knew with certainty that this was what her mother had in mind. She had the examination immediately and a small cancer was found that was easily removed with surgery. She had been unaware of the melanoma on her back. The cancer would likely have spread by the time that she had discovered it on her own. The warning from her mother had saved her life!

A warning from a dead mother saved another person from a car accident. As a man was driving his usual path to work, he distinctly "heard" his mother (who had died two years before) tell him to take another route. Feeling a bit foolish, he did take another route. Later in the day, he heard on the news that there had been a ten-car pileup in the fog right where he would have been that morning had he not taken the alternate route.

Another man was saved from a fatal accident by his deceased son. One day as he was approaching a railroad track, he was deep in thought until he heard his son say very clearly, "Watch out, Dad!" He turned toward the voice just in time to see an approaching train. He just had time to stop and was not injured at all. At that same moment, his wife suddenly sensed that he was in danger; she was very relieved when he arrived home shortly thereafter.

These are dramatic examples of visitations from dead relatives that save people from imminent danger. While these are fascinating and dramatic stories, the more common experience is that a person just "feels" the presence of their loved one on occasion. There may not be any particular warning or message, but just a feeling of warmth and connectedness. My belief is that most people have that kind of connection with a deceased loved one at some time in their lives. However, even though people may feel loved ones around them after their deaths, I think that at some other level these deceased loved ones are continuing their journeys even if they are being present to some extent for the remaining loved ones.

CHAPTER 8

Relationship Between NDEs
and Other Mystical Experiences:
Two Types of Spiritual Awakening

⇥ FROM the first talk that I gave on near-death experiences, it became clear to me that many people have experiences that are mystical in nature and don't have a place where they can feel comfortable discussing their experiences. They are very puzzled and have many questions about the experiences. These people seldom say anything during the question-and-answer part of my talks, but frequently come up to me afterwards and tell me about their experiences. When I began to formulate my ideas about a group for exploring the NDE, I realized that I would like to make it also available for people who have had mystical experiences that are not associated with physiologic compromise.

From listening to many people's stories, I've come to some conclusions. First, and most important, is that NDEs and mystical experiences are two avenues to the experience of being in the presence of God. One is not more important than the other. They are just different paths. Each is a type of spiritual awakening. Second, it is easier for some people to dismiss their mystical experiences as just an unusual event than it is for those who have had an NDE to do so. I have, however, known people who dismissed their NDEs (on a conscious level, anyway) and others who have used a mystical experience as a springboard to a whole new way of looking at the world. Lastly, it is often difficult to differentiate between a mystical experience and an

NDE. Sometimes the mystical experience occurs in a terminally-ill patient who has weeks or months to live. In those cases, it is merely by definition that they might not also be considered an NDE. Several stories will illustrate these points.

One young man related a story that occurred during a near-accident on the freeway. As a truck veered toward his car, he had a flash of pure panic as he realized that he had nowhere to go to get out of its way because of the heavy freeway traffic. It flashed through his mind that he was much too young to be dying this way. In the next moment, he had a feeling of absolute calm and peace as he realized that he was a soul that had existed before this lifetime and that would exist after this body had died. He felt surrounded by God and at perfect peace about whatever was about to happen. The truck swerved back into its lane just in time to avoid hitting his car and there was not an accident. However, this young man's life was quite changed. Since that episode, he has had an entirely new view of life. He doesn't take the "small" things of life so seriously; for him, life is a long stretch of time that doesn't include just his years here on Earth in his present body. He feels that he gets more joy out of life as a result of the experience. Certainly his spiritual awakening resulted in many of the changes that are seen in the lives of people who have had NDEs.

In contrast, a high-powered executive told about an experience that she had on her way to work one day. As she drove her usual freeway to work, she suddenly felt as if she were in the presence of God. In that experience, she understood that we are all intimately connected with one another and that when anything happens to anyone, it affects the whole planet. She had never thought about the unity of all life, being a competitive business woman. Shortly there-after she arrived at work and quickly picked up her old style of thinking and behaving.

She thought that she had forgotten the experience until she listened to an NDE talk, when her experience came back to her with perfect clarity. In discussing her experience, she felt that the ideas were so discordant with how she behaved and thought, that her subconscious was anxious to bury it as soon as possible. She also speculated that it was easier to bury the experience because she went directly to work and continued her usual daily activities. Had a similar experience occurred during an NDE when she was injured or ill, she would have been required by her physical circumstances to lie in bed for a while and think about the experience without other things to distract her. She feels that that would have made a big difference in the integration of the experience into her thinking and values.

It seems to me that there must be some interplay between our personalities and how we integrate the experience into our lives. One scientist shared a story similar to the businesswoman's, but his response to the mystical experience was much more of a spiritual awakening.

Prior to the experience, the scientist was a confirmed atheist. He felt certain that when we die, all that was us returns to the earth. In his spontaneous mystical experience, he suddenly understood the Universe and knew that it is all unfolding in exactly the way that it needs to unfold for understanding to develop. He could see how everything relates to everything else and how truly beautiful and intricate that it all is. When the experience was over, he was a changed man. He found it so wonderful and surprising that he wanted to share it with everyone that he knew.

Since most of his friends had belief systems like his earlier one, he met a great deal of skepticism. Those friends have gradually faded from his life, to be replaced with new friends with belief systems more similar to the one he now espouses. His interests have changed so dramatically since the spiritual awakening that he just doesn't have much in common with his old friends. As a result of the experience, he also developed a newfound psychic sensitivity to the emotions of others. It took some time for him to learn when to share what he was intuiting from other people and when to use discernment and remain silent. He relayed some stories of when he would have done well to have thought before he spoke!

⊰ ONE woman was perfectly healthy when she asked from the depths of her soul what it meant to follow God. To her surprise, she heard that it meant to love her children unconditionally, even her adult son who was an alcoholic. That felt to her like a very difficult task, as her reaction to his addiction had been to distance herself from him. However, understanding it as the will of God and the order of things, she made a tremendous effort not only to appear loving, but to *be* loving. Because of her unconditional love, her son was able to change his lifestyle.

⇥ SEVERAL people have shared experiences that have occurred to them in the midst of deep depressions. These experiences seemed to be gifts to help them in their darkest moments.

One man told of a time when he was very depressed, seeing a psychiatrist, and taking anti-depressant medications. One day in therapy he said he felt that God punished people who tried to commit suicide. His therapist looked surprised and asked, "You don't believe in God, do you?" He thought that over for the rest of the day and decided to kill himself that night. If there wasn't a God to punish him, he felt as though he would like to stop his life right then.

As he prepared to take an overdose of anti-depressant medication, he suddenly found himself out of his body and in the presence of the infinite love of God. In that presence he understood that he was here to learn about love and that suicide would keep him from learning what he needed to learn. After that, he never seriously considered suicide again. His recovery process from the depression was greatly facilitated by the experience.

Another woman described a very negative encounter during a depressive episode. She was already feeling very discouraged when someone told her that she ought to kill herself because she was of no use to anyone. That evening as she was recalling the encounter, she suddenly found herself surrounded by a peaceful white light that seemed to imply that she was very much worth having around. She said that the experience was very unexpected and unbidden on a conscious level. It was a life-changing event for her, however, and she has never felt so despondent since.

In contrast to that woman's spontaneous experience of the presence of light, a man told of his fervent prayer for God to show himself when he was in the midst of deep despair. He cried out for God to show himself if he existed at all. To his utter joy, he suddenly experienced himself being bathed in the Light.

Another man told of a similar story. He recently had been discharged from nine months in a mental hospital for suicidal depression. Shortly after coming home, his companion left him, he was withdrawn from his anti-anxiety medications, and he was feeling absolutely bereft. In his despair, he lay down one night with his hands in a praying position and asked for God to be his companion since it didn't appear that he was to have human companions. He fell asleep and was awakened two hours later by a mystical experience. A golden shaft of light beamed down through the middle part of his body. It felt to him as though it had come directly from God. His arms lifted into the Light of their own accord. He felt that he had seen Jesus. Ever after, he remembered that moment and felt safe and loved in the arms of Jesus. When he told me of his experience some twenty years after its occurrence, the light and joy in his eyes were as if it had just happened. It was a true spiritual awakening, even though it didn't involve any physiologic compromise at all! As a result of the experience, he was able to go on with his life. He became a much-loved teacher.

⊰⊱ SOMETIMES mystical experiences have occurred in the midst of terrifying circumstances. One young man told the story of an abduction by an escaped convict. He was in his early twenties when he was forced at gun point to stay with the convict fleeing from the police. He thought for several days that he would be killed by the convict or by the police. At the end of the adventure, as they were in a high-speed chase, he was certain that he would either be shot by accident or be killed when the car crashed.

The next thing that he knew, however, was that he was out of his body and in a tunnel with a bright light. He felt that supportive beings were present, but didn't really see anyone. It was the most peaceful experience he had ever had.

He said that he felt that he was supposed to live to accomplish something but still isn't sure what that something is. While he was having his experience, the convict decided to give himself up and stopped the car. The young man was not injured in the least, although it did take years of counseling for him to recover from the psychological trauma of those few days.

These spiritual awakenings seem to happen to people from all walks of life, and they seem to come bidden and unbidden. One man shared a profound experience that he had one evening in a bar after completing final examinations that day. He and a fellow student were relaxing with a drink when they were surprised to see a young woman walk in with a dulcimer. She seemed to be lightly attired for the northern climate. She sat down and played three songs, the last of which was an obscure sixteenth-century folk song that had been a favorite of his deceased father. As she sang it, he felt that his father spoke to him to reassure him that he had done well on his tests and that he was always watching over him. After the third song, the young woman left. Both young men were amazed at her brief presence and the evening started the story teller on a lifelong spiritual journey. He began to see a divine order to life that he had never appreciated before.

A man's experience helped him deal with his chronic illness and fear of death. Shortly after being diagnosed with emphysema and told that it would eventually lead to his death, he had a dream that didn't feel like a dream to him. He "dreamed" that he was dying and was being sucked down through fog and quicksand. It was very frightening, particularly as it had some of the components of the shortness of breath and suffocation that he felt when his lung disease was out of control. However, in his dream he emerged from the fog and quicksand into a beautiful spacious place with lovely pastels and blues where he was allowed to float with ease. From there he entered a tunnel and saw a light ahead of him. As he was drawn toward the light, he heard a voice tell him that he would go back for a while, but that "they" just wanted him to know how it was going to be. After the experience, he felt much more relaxed about dying and about living.

A woman told about an experience that was very typical for an

NDE—including the tunnel, the life review, and the Being of Light. However, she wasn't near death. She was in a time in her life when she was "partying a lot" but life was feeling very meaningless. She had her experience in the middle of a crowded bar with several friends around her. It had the same effect on her as an NDE has on people who have them. She quickly gave up the drinking and the partying and began a spiritual search which has continued to the present day.

One man told of mystical experiences that seem to have come at crucial points in his life. He is by style a rough-hewn man who owns and operates a business.

His first experience occurred in his teens, when he felt that he was suddenly in the presence of God which manifested itself as Light. It was beautiful and profound, but he never told anyone about the experience. Some twenty years later, he was questioning the meaning of life when he said to himself that he would have to die to find out, but that he wasn't ready for that! However, to his surprise, in the next moment he felt that he did "die" and he found himself being carried "beyond the border." In that place, he found that all of us are One, including the plants, rocks, and animals. There was no evil, but only good people who were confused but who would still return to the Great Oneness. He knew that the purpose of being here is to learn to be loving.

He says that, while that experience was very moving to him, he doesn't feel that it really changed how he lived his life. He only understood at that point that the competitive, hard way that he lives his life is probably not what God intended; so the experience really introduced more dissonance into his life.

His most recent experience occurred soon after the birth of his daughter. At that time, he asked God why he had been given a daughter; to his surprise, he heard the answer that his heart is hard and that a daughter has been given to him to teach him how to love. This is his only child and the joy of his life. He feels that he hasn't yet changed the way that he lives, but now he knows that there is another way. I suspect that he has some more mystical experiences ahead of him in this lifetime.

A woman told of a similar incident that occurred at the end of a week-long workshop on death and dying. At the end, several of the participants lifted her up with their fingertips. As she felt herself lifted by these loving people, she suddenly found herself out of her body, watching the scene below. She felt herself surrounded by God's love in a very mystical way. That experience had a profound influence on her life and was certainly a spiritual awakening for her. Her experience has totally removed her fear of dying. She also devotes much of her time to volunteer work.

⇥ NOT all mystical awakenings happen to adults. Some people tell of experiences that occurred during their childhoods as well.

One woman talked about just such an experience that occurred when she was a nine-year-old girl. One day she had a strong sense that she was going to see Jesus that night. As she expected, that evening she saw his face and it was the most radiant loving face that she could possibly imagine. That experience has influenced her to this day. She has become a nurse and feels very fulfilled in her work.

An elderly gentleman with a neurological disease so severe that he couldn't lift a finger, told me of a profound experience he had as a five-year-old that had greatly influenced his life. In the experience, he felt that he was in the presence of God and that everything was just the way that it was supposed to be. He said that since that moment, he has never doubted that his life was under guidance by God and that everything that has ever happened to him was perfect—including the neurological disorder that led to his being unable to move at all. That experience and his complete faith in the experience had made his life much easier for him than if he had railed against the illness.

One of the first memories of another man was from when he was four years old. He stated that he lived on a farm in the Northeast and was always fascinated with animal tracks in the mud. On the particular day of the incident, he was following such a track when he paid no attention to the fact that he was leaving the field and entering the dirt road. It was not a heavily traveled road, but a big truck came over the hill as the tiny four-year-old entered the road, partially lost in a truck tire track. He looked up just as the truck was approaching him. He stated that he had an out of body experience of looking down on the little boy about to be hit by the truck. He experienced a moment of complete tranquillity as he realized that he would be just fine even if he were killed by the truck. The truck swerved at the last minute and he was not harmed at all. Since that time, he has felt a strong spiritual connection.

➻ WITH regard to the continuum between mystical experiences and NDEs in terminally-ill patients, two examples will help to illustrate the difficulty in differentiating between these two types of experiences.

One woman who was dying of pancreatic cancer told of an experience that had occurred a year before she was diagnosed with cancer. While in the midst of a prayer circle with a group of women, she felt that she was in the presence of Jesus. Several times after that she had felt his presence. As she lay dying from the cancer, she remembered those experiences and said that she was ready to die. She didn't know whether or not she had undiagnosed cancer at the time of the first mystical experience, but she was enormously grateful for the experiences as they made her last months of life so much easier for her.

A forty-year-old woman had an out-of-body experience one month before dying from cancer. In that experience, the found herself in the presence of pure Light and Peace. She felt that she had the opportunity to die then, but chose to stay because of her husband and unfinished business. After the experience, each day she would make a list of things to do and would accomplish what she could. As the next two weeks progressed, the lists got shorter and shorter each day. Her lists included items such as visits with old friends, as well as teaching her husband how to iron his shirts and cook his meals. Finally, there were no more lists. One day, she was quite restless when she seemed to be reliving all of the experiences of her life. As night fell, she told her husband that it had been one of the best days of her life. After reviewing it all, there was nothing that she would have done differently. In that peaceful knowledge, she relaxed into a deep sleep and died peacefully two days later.

⊰| |⊱

ALTHOUGH I have primarily discussed mystical awakenings that have come unbidden or nearly spontaneously, there is a long tradition of spiritual seekers working very hard to achieve these episodes of enlightenment. This has gone on in all cultures and traditions.

It is a common practice in the East, for example, to meditate and fast for long periods with the hope of receiving an experience such as the ones described above. That is also common in the Native American tradition, with the sweat lodges and vision quests. Several people have told me of experiencing Oneness with God and all that is through such intense spiritual practices. One man said that he has had several such experiences as a result of his meditative practices.

A word of caution, however: Spiritual teachers are clear that mystical experiences are not the goal of the practice. The meditation is practiced for its own sake in order to calm the mind and to learn focusing. If a mystical experience happens, it is a blessing, but it is not the goal of the meditation and the meditation is not a failure if the mystical experience doesn't occur. Unlike much of what we Westerners believe about the working of the world, this sort of experience is beyond our control. The gradual development of a spiritual awareness is certainly available through effort, with some grace thrown in for good measure, but a spiritual awakening remains a gift and a blessing.

CHAPTER 9

Long-term Effects of NDEs

⇥ IF there were no long-term effects of NDEs, they would still be interesting and important; but I think that the long-term effects are their most significant aspect, both to the person who had the experience and for what they tell about the purpose of Earth experience.

In our NDE support group, it was essentially universal that people took years to integrate the experience. One young man talked about how much he enjoyed his life before he had an NDE during a motorcycle accident. He was a typical twenty-year-old who very much enjoyed drinking with the guys, having as many girlfriends as possible, and doing the bare minimum of work to stay in college. Suddenly, after his NDE, he no longer enjoyed those activities as much. He went through a difficult questioning period: His joy in his old lifestyle was definitely missing, but nothing had come along to replace it. He found himself bored with the topics of conversation that had been so interesting before. His friends gradually drifted away as the discrepancies in their interests became apparent. For quite a while, he felt adrift—no longer satisfied with his old lifestyle, essentially without friends, yet not able to connect with a new, more satisfying lifestyle.

He took a few months off from school to be alone and to re-integrate who he was. During that time, he went to a counselor who was aware of the impact of NDEs on people's lives. When he re-entered college, he changed his major from business to social work and met new friends who shared his new, more philosophical interests. When he came to our NDE group, he was just about to finish his degree and was quite happy with his new lifestyle and friends; but he remembered those two years of integration as very unhappy years.

His story was a happy one, but many people are not so fortunate as to be at a place in life where it is easy to change majors and make new friends. Those kinds of changes are much more difficult for people who are more established in a lifestyle and setting that involves other people.

One man told of how his NDE affected his career. Prior to the NDE, he was a very successful car salesman—the top salesperson in his region, and known for his ability to "sell anybody anything." He approached his job with great zeal and often put in 70–80 hour work weeks. After his NDE and the physical recovery process from the car accident, he was appalled at his lack of enthusiasm at work.

For the first time, when he showed a potential customer a new car, he found himself considering if this was the right car for them. Was it truly an affordable car for this person? On reflection, he discovered that his attitude now was that he wanted to make the perfect match between the customer and the car—not so much to make a sale as to help the customer select a good means of transportation that was in his or her price range. Whereas his past pattern of salesmanship had been to sell the most expensive model with the most options that he could convince the customer that he needed, now he really listened to what the customer *said* he needed and tried to provide that model with those options. In fact, sometimes he convinced the potential customer that he really didn't need a new car at all, but had just been dazzled by advertisements.

This change in his selling habits certainly did result in a lower income than he had previously earned with commissions, but he realized that he could no longer do harm to the customers and feel good about it. Before his NDE, he had the highest sales in the region; but he also had the highest rate of repossessions, because his customers had tended to buy automobiles that they couldn't really afford. Now he had very satisfied customers with payments they really could afford. He was content with his lower income because he felt like a partner with the customer, sharing common goals. The lower income was somewhat difficult for him, but he understood that the new approach to salesmanship was essential as a result of his NDE.

Other people have had more difficulty re-fashioning their lives after an NDE when families are involved. One career army man found his life totally disrupted by his NDE and the changes in his attitudes that it spawned. He had been so successful in the army and had moved steadily up the ranks because he was known as a good soldier and an excellent fighter. After the NDE, he no longer wanted to be transferred to the front lines. He knew that his promotions depended on his performance "in the field," but he found himself having nightmares about the people that he had killed during his career and worrying about what had become of their families after the deaths of the men. Life had been so simple before! He had followed orders and not given it another thought. Now he had all of these haunting memories and concerns.

When his thoughts and concerns didn't change after several months, he decided to leave the army as soon as possible even though he had been in the service for seventeen years. His wife and children were appalled, as they liked their lives as part of the army community. He had been promoted over the years and his wife enjoyed her position as the spouse of an advanced officer. Nothing could dissuade him, however, and he did not re-enlist when his next opportunity arose.

Over the next year or two, the family had some very hard times— from being severely limited financially and from the loss of their social support system when he left the army. His wife couldn't tolerate their new lifestyle, obtained a divorce, and entered the work force for the first time in her life. Since her only previous occupation had been as the wife of an army officer, her lack of education and experience in any particular field caused her great difficulties in finding work. He went to school and became a physical therapist. Though he never achieved his previous level of income and prestige, he was much happier in his new profession.

Being unconcerned about money is typical of people who have had NDEs, but that lack of concern rarely extends to the rest of the family. Family members are accustomed to a certain lifestyle and, without the benefit of the insights of the NDE, a change to a less affluent lifestyle often feels like an unnecessary deprivation. This can cause enormous conflict in the family, as the family members feel cheated by the change in values of the breadwinner who had an NDE. If all parties involved don't deal with the clash in values with patience and understanding, it is not unusual for the conflict to end in divorce. In fact, it is my impression that divorce is much more common among people who have had NDEs than among the population at large. Attitudes toward economics play a large part in the divorce rate, but attitudes toward love are probably even more important.

The main message of the NDE is that we have been born on Earth in order to learn how to love well. When people undergo a life review, each instant in their lives is reviewed, not just the "big" ones. They find that it matters how they treat people in the grocery line or on the freeway. In the life review, they often re-experience the event, both from their own perspective and from the perspective of the person with whom they were interacting. Hence, if they were unkind, they feel how it felt to the other person. Having an experience like that really lets a person feel how connected we all really are.

Even for people who don't have a classical life review, there is still an experience of what absolute unconditional love feels like, and it is addictive. Once having felt it, people want to experience it and to give it more and more. Hence, people who have had NDEs often have difficulties with boundary issues. When they relate with another person, they feel what that person feels and have great empathy with them. As a result, they tend to give a lot more of their time and energy to people outside of the family and their immediate circle of friends; that can create stresses in their private lives, particularly if the family feels that they are getting less of the person because he or she is giving more to relative strangers.

In talking with many people who have had NDEs, I find that this is almost a universal problem. Whether or not it becomes an insurmountable problem in the family depends on two things. First is the ability of the person with the NDE to consider the effect of his or her actions on the family. While that person will never again have the same attitudes as before the NDE, he or she can moderate their behavior to some extent. The second factor is the family's ability to change their expectations of the person who has had the NDE. If the family can give him or her space to give more to other people, they can all settle into a new way of being that is often more comfortable and loving than the environment that they had before the NDE.

Another factor that bears heavily on how a person adjusts to an NDE is the people whom they tell. Several people have shared with me horrendous occurrences that happened because they told the wrong person about their experience. In the past, when people told their doctors about their experiences, doctors unaware about the existence of NDEs have felt that this kind of experience must fall in the realm of the psychiatrist. These people were often referred to psychiatrists who either gave them medications which dulled their new-found sensitivities and/or labeled them as having a psychiatric disturbance. With that diagnosis, the thrust of psychotherapy was to convince them that their NDE was not "real," but a psychiatric aberrancy. In fact, in the past, people have been hospitalized in a psychiatric ward as a result of having told their physicians about the NDE. Making sense of the experience was very much confounded by psychiatric input from the medical community. Hopefully, that sort of occurrence is a thing of the past, but it was devastating to the people to whom it happened.

Another common thing that has happened to people who have told their doctors is that they have been referred to clergy who know as little about NDEs as doctors do. Clergymen often dismissed the experience out-of-hand or, worse, saw it as the work of the devil, no matter how positive the experience was. That kind of response adds a whole new layer of adjustment issues. Hopefully that also is a problem that is rapidly dissolving as information continues to pour forth about NDEs.

One clergyman recently told me that the Church is going to have to adapt to the fact of NDEs because the congregations are demanding it. I feel the same way about the medical community. When people from all walks of life come to understand that NDEs are extraordinarily common when people are close to dying or resuscitated, clergy and physicians will have to shift their own paradigms to accommodate them.

Clergyman and physicians are not the only ones that have caused people to suppress their NDEs, however. Frequently, parents have told children who tried to share their NDEs that they were hallucinating or dreaming. This has also been true of spouses and friends.

It is very important to whom the person first tells their experience. If that person is accepting, the person with the NDE feels more confident about telling others. Negative responses that come later are not nearly so important as the first responses, when the experience is still fresh in his or her mind. In contrast, if that first telling of the experience is met with a negative response, the person often refrains from telling the story for years and years and may even repress it themselves.

It seems to me that people who tell no one about the experience adjust better to it than those who tell someone who gives them a negative response. In my own experience as a child, I remember choosing to tell no one about the experience because I didn't feel that anyone I knew would be able to understand it and I feared that it would frighten them and make them think that they would need to "fix" me in some way. Having not risked telling the story, I have no real idea of what the response might have been.

My experience occurred in 1950. At a talk in 1993, I was struck with just how much attitudes toward NDEs have changed over the last few years. One woman said of her experience some thirty years ago that she had never told a single soul because of her fear that people would think that she was "crazy." After that talk, a young man expressed his annoyance at some of his friends because they felt that he talked about his NDE *too much* of the time. They had apparently been interested in hearing the experience at first; but they wanted to talk about other things more than he did, and he just didn't understand why they weren't as taken with the experience as he was. What a difference a few years has made!

➳ WHEN talking about long-term effects of NDEs, it is important to talk about the chronic "homesickness" that people who have had NDEs share. Whenever a group gets together, the difficulties of adjusting are discussed; but sooner or later, someone always mentions how wonderful it was and how much they are looking forward to being there again when this life is over. It is universally understood that it is not a good thing to hasten that process through suicide or neglect of our bodies, but all NDErs are a little homesick.

One of the most dramatic examples of this homesickness that I have experienced was an encounter with one of our hospice patients. She was a woman in her thirties, dying of cancer, who had devoted her life after her NDE to helping other people. One evening in our in-patient unit, she asked me to sit with her a while. She shared that she felt she would be dying very soon and wanted to discuss some things with me.

We first talked about her finishing up the business details of her life. She was very lucid and it was clear that all of those business details were completed. We then talked about her regrets about leaving her young husband as a widower. Having discussed the important things of this world, she then said that she understood her time on Earth was in God's hands and that she was really looking forward to going home again. As the sun sank and the sky darkened outside her room, she spoke of the love and contentment that she had felt during her NDE. Her face glowed as she remembered that time and acknowledged that she would be there again soon. I shared my experience with her and the feeling that that was the most perfect time I have had since I was born here. It was an evening of shared nostalgia.

The next morning, she slipped into a coma from which she did not awaken. She died peacefully two days later with a smile on her lips. I have always been grateful that I took the time that evening to stay with her a while, although I had no idea at the time that it was her last lucid day.

Sometimes the nostalgia of the NDE can be very helpful. One woman said that she had been in the habit of telling herself that she could just kill herself if things got too bad. After this kind of mind-talk for several years, she did finally attempt suicide. During the suicide attempt, she had an NDE in which she experienced the total love of God. In the experience, however, she got the clear impression that suicide was not "permitted."

When she was resuscitated, she felt very differently toward life. Although the same difficulties were present as before her suicide attempt, somehow they didn't loom so large as they had then. She really turned her life around.

One day, however, she again thought to herself out of habit, "If it gets too bad, I can always kill myself." In the next moment, she realized that was no longer an option for her. It was simply not permitted and she would have to find another way out of her problems. When panic began to envelop her as she considered that option closed to her, she suddenly remembered the total love that she had felt in her NDE: she knew *that* was her option when things got too difficult. She could take a breath, close her eyes, and remember that moment with nostalgia. That was reality. The rest of this life may contain problems to solve, but that love provides a solid ground of knowing where we go when we are finished with problems here.

This change in attitude after an NDE during a suicide attempt is quite common, as evidenced by the work that Bruce Greyson, M.D. has done at the University of Connecticut Medical School.[8] He is a psychiatrist who has found that people are much less likely to attempt suicide a second time if they have experienced an NDE during their first attempt. I think that this change in the suicide rate is attributable to two causes. First, people change their beliefs about what is important; often, situations that appeared to be intolerable in the past are seen in a new light. Second, there is a strong belief among suicide attempters who have undergone NDEs that suicide is not really a viable option: We are on Earth to learn lessons and checking out early is not in God's plan.

The remembrance of the NDE is also helpful in getting through life's struggles for people who have not attempted suicide. The message of the NDE is the complete oneness of all life, and it helps to feel part of that when one's own life seems to be falling apart. I had the opportunity to experience that myself when my first husband said that he wanted a divorce after ten years of marriage. Divorce was never something that I had contemplated. We had two small children, ages three and five. Having worked while my husband went to medical school, I was finally in graduate school myself at the time. He was making an income and I was thoroughly enjoying working toward a graduate degree in psychology. It was quite a blow to all of the areas of my life to suddenly be faced with a divorce.

The first evening that I knew of his decision, I was devastated and not sure how I would cope. To help myself calm down, I took the children to a park the next day. As I sat on the bench and watched them play, I suddenly found myself appreciating the sunshine and the laughter of *all* of the children, not just my own. I felt a wonderful connection with *all* of life, not just my own little segment. As I breathed in the wholeness of the moment, I knew that I would deal with the details as they came up; we would all be just fine as long as we could feel our connection with all of life.

There were difficult moments over the next several months, but that experience started me on a positive path. Because of it, I was able to ask myself what was the best possible outcome of the situation and how I could make it as positive and gentle as possible for everyone concerned. After that divorce I went to medical school, met my second husband, with whom I have a very happy marriage, and had my wonderful third child.

I honestly believe that everything that happens in life is for a purpose that will ultimately serve our highest good and that I am responsible to look for ways to be in alignment with that highest good. As I have met many people with NDEs over the past six years, I have come to realize that this attitude toward life is extremely common among people with NDEs (although, certainly, not exclusive to them).

⊰ ANOTHER long-term effect of NDEs is an increase in psychic abilities. I have seen this development particularly in people who have undergone car accidents and were comatose for long periods of time. When they awaken, they often are very psychic. This can be quite a problem, as they may find themselves blurting out something that someone else is thinking but did not plan on saying. They also frequently can foretell the future or know what is physically wrong with someone without examining them and without specific medical knowledge. I have met several of these people.

What is more common, however, is an increased sensitivity to people's feelings and moods—which can be wonderful in close relationships, but which also can cause a lot of difficulty in public settings. People who have had NDEs are often so sensitive to the energies around them that they can easily get exhausted in crowds. It is unusual, for example, for a person who has had an NDE to be comfortable shopping in crowded malls. It is as if the discordant and diverse energies of other people intrude on their own energetic space and draw from it.

By the same token, violence is very disturbing to the NDEr, even the "ordinary" violence on television or in movies. Watching the news is particularly disturbing, as all that is negative and violent is emphasized and the chaotic, painful energies of the victims somehow come across on the screen and are quite upsetting. Most people find that they simply can't watch the news for a long time after an NDE; many people choose to stop watching the news indefinitely. (My personal opinion is that brief comments on negative aspects in the world are necessary, but there is no reason to dwell exclusively on that which is violent and negative. Viewers would be better served by an emphasis on ways that people are making this a better world, than by an emphasis on the few people who are negatively impacting humanity.)

Sometimes this sensitivity is so acute that it interferes with the ability to do daily activities. Some people have difficulty holding down jobs because their minds and energies are so scattered by the violence that they see and feel. These people are often so confused and upset by the disparity that they see between the way they saw life in the NDE and the way that people treat each other in ordinary life, that they retreat into a fantasy world and refuse to venture forth into the world. Besides making their personal world uncomfortable, this response also deprives the rest of the world of one more person who understands love. It is essential for people who have had NDEs to learn how to function in the world. They are much needed.

Some people have turned to drugs and alcohol to blot out their awareness of negative energies. It is obviously not an effective coping strategy, but sometimes the pain seems too much to bear in any other way. Support groups for people who have had NDEs are very helpful for people who are too sensitive to the negative aspects of their environments. In the group, they meet other people who have gone through similar problems and they can begin to see that they will be able to modify their response to the environment enough that they will be able to cope. The sensitivity never goes away entirely, however, which is a good thing. The only way to change our world is first to become sensitized to the violence and then to do something about it, starting with changing ourselves first.

In summary, there are many long-term effects of NDEs, some of which lead to a happier, more fulfilling life, and some of which may cause considerable conflict in the lives of the people who have had them.

CHAPTER 10

Recollections of NDEs

⊸⊣ MANY people remember their NDEs from the moment that they first occurred. That was true for me, although I have gone through periods in my life when I didn't think about my NDE much at all. It is not unusual, however, to be unaware of an NDE or to misinterpret it completely.

One man didn't remember a childhood NDE until he had a second NDE as an adult. When he began having abdominal pain, he dismissed the discomfort from his mind. However, he developed a sudden increase in intensity after a couple of days and sought medical attention. His physician felt that he might have an acute appendicitis and arranged for immediate hospital admission. Before he was able to get to the operating room, he collapsed as the inflamed appendix ruptured.

As cardiopulmonary resuscitation was begun on him, he found himself drifting out of his body. Looking back on his body, he remembered that he had a similar experience years before. He said to himself, "Here I go again!" He then proceeded down a tunnel into the peaceful presence of the Being of Light. This time when he returned, he remembered both experiences.

It is not uncommon for people who have been comatose from a closed head injury to forget both an NDE and the traumatic event that precipitated it. This is particularly true if they were comatose for several days or weeks. When people undergo an injury severe enough to create a comatose state, they usually do forget the event itself. In fact, the amnesia generally extends for some time before the accident (retrograde amnesia) and for a time after the accident as well.

People with closed head injuries and unremembered NDEs go through a particularly difficult time as they recover. This is true for several reasons. First, they suffered severe head injuries or they would not have been comatose for several days. When they return to consciousness, they often have deficits in their mental capacities as well as pain in parts of their bodies from other injuries that were sustained at the time of the accident. These deficits usually include a loss of memory for a period of time, but may also involve a loss of spatial ability, visual problems, problems with speech, and so on, depending on where in the brain the injury occurred. As they gradually recover, bits and pieces of their memory return for the time around the accident; only rarely does their entire memory return. As fragments of their memory of the event return, fragments of the memory of the NDE may return as well. It is a very confusing time, with pieces of the puzzle of the last few weeks appearing out of what seems to be nowhere in a random fashion. Some people are able to remember that time in a more organized fashion if they undergo hypnotherapy. Several people have told me about remembering their NDEs under hypnosis.

One woman who was plagued by gaps in her memory surrounding the car accident that resulted in a two-month comatose episode told me of her experience with hypnosis several months after the accident. Under hypnosis, she was able to remember the entire accident, including the people who stopped along the highway and pulled her from the car. When she discussed the details with her parents, who had arrived shortly after she was taken to the hospital, they confirmed the details of what she had remembered. While remembering the accident, she also remembered her NDE, in which she watched her own body being removed from the car and then found herself in a heavenly realm. Her remembrance of that event was very important in her recovery process.

Another woman had undergone a prolonged grand mal seizure during an episode of a severe febrile illness when she was two years old. Although she was told that she was comatose for several days after the event, she didn't remember anything about the event until she underwent hypnotherapy some forty years later. At that time, she remembered being "tied down" with IV's, catheters, and so on. Then she remembered being out of her body and watching over herself as her body lay in the bed. She then remembered looking ahead and seeing a Light. She did not really go into the Light, but experienced it as very loving and very spiritual. She didn't feel that she had a choice about coming back. She remembered herself as being very sensitive and psychic as a child, and the remembrance of her NDE helped her to better understand her behavior and unusual sensitivities.

A man reported a similar increase in his understanding of himself when he was able to remember his childhood NDE during hypnotherapy. He remembered an incident when he was six years old and the garage door closed on his head. At the time of the event, he had been unconscious and hospitalized for several days. He told his mother of details that occurred during that time of unresponsiveness, but his mother told him that he was just guessing and making it up; so his young mind repressed the whole situation, including the NDE. It was not until he underwent hypnotherapy twenty years later that he remembered the events surrounding the accident. At the time that he told me the story, he was still working with the memories—some two years after he had first begun to remember them.

⇥ IN some ways, the recovery and adjustment process is more difficult for people who don't remember their NDEs. They find themselves with the same changes in their value systems as other people who have had NDEs, but they have no idea as to why they are suddenly so changed. I have had people tell me that after a serious accident they just weren't interested in going back to their previous careers, particularly if they didn't see those careers as being generally helpful to humanity. They also frequently find themselves appalled by violence of any kind. Watching the evening news on television becomes impossible. Concern over material possessions becomes a thing of the past.

On the surface, these changes in attitude may appear to be as a result of a close brush with death, not necessarily an NDE. While that may be partially true, Dr. Melvin Morse has shown in his book, *Closer to the Light,* that children with serious life-threatening illnesses didn't have a permanent change in their values unless they also had an NDE.[9] That has been my observation as well. A person who nearly dies may see a change in attitude for a few weeks or months, but will fairly quickly drift back into old attitudes unless he or she also had an NDE. These changes are especially puzzling to people who don't remember their NDE.

One example of a woman who doesn't remember her NDE, but who has all of the characteristics of a person who has had one, is a young woman who suffered from anorexia and bulimia (eating disorders) in her teens. She remembers feeling very faint and weak while out with friends. According to her friends, she then had a seizure, but she doesn't remember anything of that night beyond feeling very weak. (It is not unusual for people with severe eating disorders to develop a metabolic imbalance that leads to seizures.) Since that night, her behavior and values have changed dramatically, although she doesn't remember an NDE. She is no longer so concerned about her body-image or her clothes. She has become much calmer and introspective. Her interests in being of help to other people and in education have greatly increased. She feels that she was incredibly self-centered and selfish prior to the event.

Without a remembrance of the NDE, people often think that they are "going crazy" when they can no longer predict how they will act in a given situation. How is it that a lucrative sales job with lots of perks no longer satisfies their souls? How is it that it is no longer fun to hang out with their buddies at the local pub and talk about sports and pick up girls? Why is it no longer satisfying to watch violent movies? Questions like these are easily answered once they remember their NDEs. When they remember that they learned that our reason for being here is to learn how to love one another, then they understand why they have changed so much and they are able to get on with their lives.

In addition to hypnotherapy as a tool to remember NDEs, sometimes a particular conversation will trigger the memory. One person told me that he was sitting in a group of people talking about NDEs. Everyone in the group was discussing their own NDEs when someone turned to him and asked why he was in the group. Without a moment's hesitation, he answered that he had had one. He was as surprised as the rest of the group when he remembered that he had had an NDE as a child.

He meditated a great deal over the next few days and the memory gradually came back to him. It had occurred in conjunction with some child abuse, so a good deal of working-through of the memories needed to take place before he could truly integrate the full experience into his life. As a result of that integration, he now works as social worker. His NDE helped him use his difficult situation as a child to help other people.

It has been rather common for people to tell me that they have remembered an NDE during the time that I was sharing other NDE stories. One particular example was an elderly lady who remembered her own near-drowning episode as a child during one of my talks.

ANOTHER group consists of people who remember NDEs but haven't recognized them for what they are. One woman in her fifties recently told me about an experience that she had some twenty years ago following an injection. After an injection of penicillin, she had a severe allergic reaction and nearly died. During the period of time when the physician was treating the reaction, she had an experience of feeling that she was out of her body and being drawn toward a Light. Afterwards, when she told the doctor about the experience, she was told that it was a dream and that she should be careful to never receive penicillin again.

She didn't think about it any more until recently when she began examining her life in more depth during counseling sessions. Because she didn't experience all of the elements described in a classical NDE, she had dismissed her experience as a dream. However, her values and attitudes are typical of people who have had an NDE, and her exploration of that aspect of her life has been very helpful in making sense of her life.

Another story told to me by a physician illustrates this as well. Years ago, during surgery for a ruptured appendix, she had a cardiac arrest. During the resuscitation, she had an experience of seeing her deceased mother and brother, both of whom seemed to reassure her that they were okay and she would be, too. She had dismissed the experience as a dream until she heard one of my talks and began to reflect on the ways that her life and attitudes had changed after the experience. In particular, she saw her profession in a whole new way and became much more humanitarian in her practice of medicine. She is an example of someone who didn't change professions, but changed the way that she did her work.

After having several people tell me of stories similar to the physician's, it occurred to me that the statistics on people who have had NDEs are probably actually too low. In a Gallup poll in 1982, one out of twenty adult Americans reported an NDE and 35% of people who had undergone a cardiac arrest reported an NDE.[10] Dr. Michael Sabom reported similar statistics when he interviewed 106 people who had survived a near-death crisis.[3] He found that 43% of them remembered an NDE. From my conversations with people over the past several years, my hunch is that more people have had NDEs than statistics indicate. They just don't always remember them, or they misinterpret them and call them something else.

CHAPTER 11

Profiles of People
Who Have Had NDEs

✥ PEOPLE from all walks of life and of all philosophical persuasions have NDEs, given the right circumstances. Several stories will illustrate this point.

One young woman told of an experience that occurred three years previously. She was taking pain pills for a broken arm when she felt faint and nauseated one evening after drinking a couple of beers. Witnesses reported that she had a grand mal seizure immediately thereafter. She doesn't remember the seizure (that is a typical characteristic of a seizure). An ambulance was called, but cardiopulmonary resuscitation was never initiated as she had stopped seizing by the time that the paramedics arrived.

Though she doesn't remember the seizure, she does remember an NDE that occurred during it. She remembers leaving her body and going to a peaceful place where she found herself on a road. As she traveled down the road, she met her mother who had died of alcoholism several years before. Her mother seemed to be there to reassure her that there was nothing to be concerned about. Her grandmother who had died was also there to reassure her. As she told me about the love and peace in that place, her eyes misted over with the remembrance. While she was appreciating her surroundings, which were lit with a soft light, she suddenly found herself slammed back into her body—as if she had been hit on the forehead by some force.

She felt that the experience was a special gift from her mother and grandmother that she needed because she had been living a rebellious and chaotic life. She thought that they wanted to show her another way of living. However, she was disappointed in herself for quite some time because she did not change her living style immediately. After the experience, she continued to live her alcoholic chaotic lifestyle for another couple of years while she integrated the experience.

Eight months before she told me her story, she had stopped drinking and had started the educational process toward her goal of becoming a physical therapist. She felt that her purpose on earth was to be helpful to other people and that she was finally on the right path. Before her experience, she had seen people as very separate from one another and very self-centered. After her experience, she saw people as very interconnected and doing the best that we can given our life circumstances. This woman had been raised a Christian and did expect that there is an afterlife, although she had not given the idea a great deal of thought in her young life prior to the NDE.

In contrast, a woman who was an atheist prior to her NDE told of a profound spiritual experience during a suicide attempt. She had been in an abusive relationship for quite some time. In the midst of a particularly violent argument, she decided that she couldn't stand it anymore and slit her wrists. Her feelings just prior to the NDE were despair and anger.

As she lost consciousness, she found herself out of her body and in a tunnel. Initially she heard the sound of bells, which soon turned to music. She then found herself in the presence of pure Light and Love and recognized that all of the things that had led to her suicide attempt were not as important as they had seemed at the time. In that moment, she understood that all that matters is love and she became a spiritual person.

Since that experience, her life has changed dramatically. She left the abusive relationship, became a much happier woman, and has never contemplated suicide again. She feels that the experience was a real gift to her to get her off a self-destructive path and into a much more peaceful and loving existence.

＊THESE experiences occur in all age groups. One middle-aged woman described an event that she remembered from her toddler stage, when she was nearly killed during an episode of child abuse. She didn't remember the event immediately, but remembered it as she underwent psychotherapy years later to help her deal with her childhood abuse. She recalled an event in which she was being choked, and was lifted out of her body into a profoundly peaceful place where she felt infinitely protected and close to God. During the experience she was told that she would always be protected and that her own angels and guides would always be around her. Since that time, she has felt them on occasion, particularly when she has been in dangerous situations, such as narrowly avoided car accidents.

One young woman told me about an experience that she had undergone when she was two years old and had remembered from the day that it happened. She said that she had been born prematurely and weighed only two pounds at birth. It was not clear for the first several months of her life if she would survive, and she was fragile and was frequently ill for her first several years. She and her mother both remember the episode from when she was two years old. At that time, she was very ill with a high fever. She felt herself go down a tunnel toward a light. Her mother remembers her sitting up in bed with a big smile on her face and reaching upward with both arms as she said, "Light." The remembrance of the feeling of joy and peace that she had during that experience has been with her since that day.

An adult physician told me of an experience that took place when he was about four years old and had an adverse reaction during a tonsillectomy. In his experience, he underwent a life review, even though that is considered uncommon in children. He reviewed all of the times that he had been unkind to his baby brother, of whom he was quite jealous. He not only remembered what he had done to his brother, but experienced the bewilderment and pain that his brother felt as the recipient of his unkind words and deeds. He said that his behavior changed temporarily as a result of the experience, but he continued to have his moments of unkindness toward his brother. The difference was that now he had some understanding of the impact on his brother and, at least, it did make him stop and think.

Another man told of an experience that occurred in a near-drowning experience when he was a five-year-old. He had remembered it since childhood. He remembers slipping into a hole in the ocean floor that had a terrific undertow. He struggled at first; but when he took his first gulp of water and felt the sea water in his nose and mouth, he suddenly lost all feeling of panic as he felt himself lifting out of his body and being surrounded by a loving Light. He felt entirely at peace with no sensation of any pain whatsoever. The next thing he remembered was the feeling of the sand grinding into his chest as someone pumped the ocean water out of his lungs. He felt perfectly miserable then, in contrast to the feeling of painless peace that he had felt the moment before. Since that time, he has devoted his life to a spiritual search and is currently part of a religious community.

One woman shared her fifteen-year-old son's NDE that occurred when he had fallen into a coma from meningitis. At the time, she was several states away on a trip, but at the moment that he fell ill she felt absolutely compelled to go home immediately. When she got home, she discovered a note on his aunt's door saying that someone had taken him to the emergency room. When she got there, the doctors told her that there was almost no chance that he would recover and if he did, he would be severely brain-damaged. In spite of all predictions, the boy awoke fully in two or three days and went on to a complete recovery.

Over the six years since the episode, he had never talked to his mother about what he had experienced while he was comatose. When she was reading a book about NDEs, it occurred to her that he might have had one during that episode. So when he next visited her home, she asked him about it. He answered in the affirmative, but said that he didn't much like to talk about it because it was so difficult to describe. When pressed, he told her that he had been in a bubble that seemed like a womb and that he just seemed to go back and back in time. He also said that it was a wonderful feeling of peace and painlessness. He hadn't specifically thought of it as an NDE, however, because it didn't involve a tunnel and he didn't see the Light. All that was typical of an NDE was the feeling of peace and painlessness.

One teen had an NDE during sodium pentothol anesthesia for wisdom teeth extraction. Although the dentist didn't tell him that anything unusual had occurred, he was unconscious for five hours. He thought that what happened was normal when a person has sodium pentothol, and was very disappointed when he had it several years later and did not repeat the experience. After he read Raymond Moody's first book, he realized that he had probably received an overdose of the medication.

In his experience, he went down a tunnel toward a bright light. There were other beings of light around, but he didn't recognize any of them. He felt himself in the presence of God while he went through the life review "like turning the pages of a book." Although he had dreaded the experience, he felt total acceptance of himself as he went through it. He did not specifically feel how his words and actions affected the other people he had been relating with. He was then told to go back "to love," and the experience was over.

⇥ SEVERAL women have talked about experiences that occurred during difficult childbirths. They generally were out of their bodies and able to observe the scene below. One woman saw her child with a cord around his neck. He was blue and she assumed that he was dead. She made the decision to turn and go down the tunnel, but somehow was slammed back into her body. To her surprise, her child was resuscitated. She felt guilty for some time afterwards about her decision to go down the tunnel, because she felt that she was being unkind toward her husband in trying to do that.

Another woman told of her awareness during her NDE that her newborn infant would die, but that the infant would be going to the Light. When her baby did die the following day, medical staff were concerned that she didn't grieve more than she did. However, she had been certain of the event from the moment of her NDE and was equally certain that her infant would be in a perfect place with no pain. While she missed him, she had confidence that all was in Divine Order. She said that the experience made it a whole lot easier for her to accept her baby's death as part of a cosmic plan rather than as a ghastly mistake.

Most commonly in childbirth, however, women decide to stay for a while to help their children to grow up. Over and over, I have heard women say that, for themselves, they wanted to stay with the Light, but their love of their children caused them to choose to come back.

⇥ ONE man relayed to me the unusual story of dual NDEs that occurred to him and a friend many years ago during the Korean War.

He was in his early twenties when his company was overrun by the enemy and bombed heavily. Only two of them remained alive and they were badly wounded. As he lay on the battlefield in agony, he suddenly found himself floating above his body in total peace and painlessness. To his surprise, when he looked around, he saw his buddy floating above his body as well. They could communicate telepathically and decided to float about the battlefield to see what else was happening. As they floated over the scene of incredible chaos and destruction, they recognized the large number of casualties, but they continued to feel at peace within themselves. They later talked about the experience as they lay in their hospital beds recovering from their massive wounds.

I wonder if simultaneous NDEs might not be that uncommon on a battlefield, where many people might well be experiencing NDEs at the same time.

The previous story refers to an NDE on the battlefield, presumably after the violence was over. Another man shared a story that took place during World War II when he was so severely wounded that a medic thought that he was dead. As they were tagging his toe to identify him as a dead man, he found himself out of his body. He tried to grab the medic, but his hand simply went through the medic's body.

At that point, he heard the medic tell the doctor that he had felt a breeze and the doctor dismissed him by saying that that was quite a common occurrence. The young soldier drew on all of his strength and moved one finger, thereby letting them know that he was indeed alive.

Meanwhile, he found himself in the presence of the brightest light, but it didn't hurt his eyes. He went through a complete life review. The he was asked, "What do you have to give?" He didn't think that he had anything to give because he was so young. His sense since then is that love is all we ever have to give. He was then asked if he wanted to go home or to stay. He loved it there, but chose to go because he felt that his mother would be too overwhelmed with sadness if her twenty-one-year-old son died.

◄ᴴ FROM these profiles, it is clear that NDEs occur in all age groups, that they happen to people from all walks of life and with all types of belief systems, and that they occur in all kinds of situations where the body is near death. In fact, the latter is the only common denominator.

CHAPTER 12

Toward a Void or Toward the Link?

⊰ IN the many hundreds of NDEs that have been told to me, only a few were negative; but these have chilling implications about the meaning of separation and isolation. No one has told me of a typical "hellfire and damnation" type of experience, but I have heard three episodes of feelings of profound separation.

One young man had prolonged seizures after an overdose of drugs. He found himself in an environment that he described as a "Void." As far as he could see, the atmosphere was entirely a dingy gray with no relief to its monotony. Nothing was visible at all except for a disc that was nearby. That disc was black on one side and white on the other. It turned back and forth very slowly. With each reversal, there was a clicking sound. That sound was the only sound, and the turning of the disc was the only movement in the environment. He felt totally isolated, totally alone in that heavy gray void. He felt that this same scene would go on for a very long time, perhaps even eternity.

As the feeling of isolation became unbearable, he realized that the life that he had been leading before that night had been inexorably moving in that direction. This "Void" was the ultimate outcome of a life filled with drugs to produce isolation, a circle of "friends" whose only interest was in acquiring drugs, and a lack of concern for other people as he preyed on them to get the money to pay for the drugs. He knew in every fiber of his being such intense separation was not what he wanted.

With the loneliness of this void all around him and the incessant clicking sound in the background, he cried out in desperation, "God, help me!" With that cry from the depths of his soul, he found himself back in his body. With abiding gratitude for his release from the void, he began a different path, although it was not always easy.

The old environment was still there. Only he was changed. He gradually gave up the drugs and, with them, the old friends who hadn't changed. He became a spiritual seeker and found that all of the world's religions emphasize the ways that we are connected to each other. He began to look for ways to be helpful to other people instead of ways to take advantage of them. Though he didn't always live it in every moment, as none of us do, he had indeed discovered that love is the link, and he never forgot it.

Another separation-type experience was told by a middle-aged man who recounted a chilling experience from some twenty years prior during a motorcycle accident. He remembers leaving his body after the impact and then nearly being sucked down a tunnel by very powerful forces. He was surrounded by a sickly yellow-green light. He was certain that if he let himself be sucked down the tunnel he would surely die. It was terrifying to the young man, but he summoned all of his strength and began to claw his way up the tunnel. After what seemed hours, he finally made it to the top of the tunnel and his experience was over. He feels that he saved his own life that day. He may well be correct on that; but by insisting on being separate and doing it all himself, he may have kept himself from the more typical NDE that usually starts in a tunnel that is dark and frightening at first, but gives way to the presence of the Being of Light and an incredible feeling of peace. We'll never know. In any event, his experience has been influential in how he lives his life in that he tends to hold himself aloof from other people and to rely very much on himself and on his own capabilities.

Supporting the importance of a person's interpretation of an experience is a similar experience told to me by two different people, but interpreted in very different ways. During the experience, both people found themselves transported into space. They both felt that they were in the darkness of space, wandering among the stars. It was a very still environment.

One woman was terrified. She was very much afraid that she would be lost and wouldn't be able to return to Earth. Her only memory of the experience is the fear that she felt: She just wanted it to be over.

In contrast, the other woman was fascinated by her similar experience. As she floated among the stars, she felt herself connected to the whole Universe. That feeling of connection with the Universe was incredibly satisfying and peaceful to her. She saw that the little problems of her life that sometimes loomed so large were quite insignificant in the grand scheme of things. Her view of the world was greatly expanded by the experience, and she speaks of it with awe and wonder. It started her on a path of seeking connection with nature and with other human beings.

Those three negative stories are the only ones that I have personally been told. However, one man did share with me that his father had a look of horror on his face when he died. He had led a lonely, angry life and he died embittered toward nearly everyone. It is impossible to know whether he saw something horrible at death or only realized that this life is not all that there is and feared what lay ahead. Either thing might have been quite frightening to him. We will never know, of course. It is interesting to me, however, that I have never seen anyone die with a look of horror.

On reflection on the meaning of what the young man on drugs called a "Void," it becomes clear that we experience something that is appropriate to call a Void in many settings, long before we encounter it in an NDE. One of the opportunities of the dying process is to become aware of this Void and to move away from it. There are several ways that we create such a Void in our lives. One way to do that is, of course, by the use of drugs. But there are many other ways to create that Void, including living a life filled with only the superficial, living a life as a workaholic, and keeping people away with anger or fear, to mention just a few examples. The process of dying sometimes gives people the opportunity to re-evaluate such attitudes and to change them. Of course, people also have the option of remaining exactly as they have been.

ONE elegantly dressed, beautiful young woman was appalled when her middle-aged, handsome, executive husband was told that the lump in his mouth was cancerous. After extensive surgery that left him slightly disfigured, they were able to return to much of their former life—until they discovered that the surgery and the radiation treatments had not been enough to keep the cancer from growing. Over the next several months, they tried chemotherapy, but the mass continued to grow. When it was obvious to everyone that no more active treatment would be helpful, they sought hospice care.

When I first met her, this beautiful young wife was sitting on her pristine white couch in her living room, surrounded by the beautiful things that they had collected over the ten years that they had been together. Each thing was perfect and very carefully placed in their expensive, beautiful home. Although she had every hair in place and was wearing the perfect accessories for her very stylish at-home clothes, I sensed that underneath the facade she was crumbling.

When she asked what to expect of the next few weeks, I assured her that we would do everything that we could do to control her husband's pain and secretions (he continually drooled because of the massive tumor in his mouth), but that there might be considerable bleeding if the tumor eroded into a large blood vessel. Trembling, she looked about the room, and I could see she was imagining what that would be like in her well-ordered existence.

Over the next few weeks, her husband did decline rapidly. He was no longer the one who made all of the decisions, but gradually withdrew from his interest in the details of life as his tumor progressed. He no longer wanted to get dressed in the morning and, finally, didn't even want to get out of bed at all. He lost weight as his tumor grew larger and more disfiguring.

With each change in her husband, it was as if the young woman's world crumbled a little more. She talked with her social worker about how she had married into a lifestyle that she really wanted with interesting witty friends, dinners at good restaurants, and trips around the world. They had only been married seven years when the nightmare with the cancer began. It just wasn't fair, she railed. As he became sicker and needed more care just to swallow liquids or to go to the bathroom, she became more bitter. She began to wish for it to be over so that she could resume her life. She felt angry with him for not keeping his part of their bargain. She was beautiful, witty, and well-kept—the perfect complement to a wealthy business executive. How *dare* he become disfigured with cancer, lose all his money paying for the treatments that didn't cure him anyway, and now become someone that needed care day and night!

In her bitterness and anger, she had moved to the guest room several weeks before the night that she thought that she heard someone knocking on her wall at 2 A.M. She was several rooms away from her husband and didn't think that she could hear him knock on the wall that far away. In fact, he had a buzzer to ring if he needed her. She listened again and, while she didn't hear anything that time, she had the strong sense that her husband needed her. At first she tried to ignore the feeling and go back to sleep, but it was impossible, so she got up to check on him.

When she arrived in his room, she found that he was still conscious, but his breathing pattern had changed dramatically. His breath was coming in uneven sighs. He whispered to her that he was dying. Her eyes grew large and she immediately thought of calling the hospice nurse. As she started to go to the phone, he said, "Please stay with me," with pleading in his eyes. At his request, she lay down with him and held him. He relaxed into her arms.

As she held him and listened to his breathing becoming slower and shallower through the long night, she felt her own heart melting. For the first time, she allowed herself to feel how much she loved this man. In her heart, she felt their soul connection. He was no longer a handsome, rich, successful businessman who was a good partner, but he was simply someone she really loved. As she lay there stroking him, she looked back over the times that he had tried to tell her of his deep love for her. She had glossed over it at the time, but now realized that he had loved her in that way all along. He recognized the outer beauty and the polished veneer, but his heart had always responded to a place in her that she was barely aware of at all. His last gift to her was to help her see that core of herself that he had always loved and to give her one last chance to let her heart open. She was oblivious to the drooling and the oozing blood as she looked into the peaceful face of the loved husband who was dying in her arms.

As the sky began to lighten outside of the window, he opened his eyes and whispered, "I love you, baby." While holding him tenderly with her arms and legs entwined around his, she whispered back, "I love you too, baby—and thank you." He died in the next few moments, still in her arms.

When she called the hospice nurse a few minutes later, her voice was full of wonder and calmer than her nurse had ever heard it before. She had just spent the most remarkable night of her life and she would never again be quite the same person as she had been just four hours ago. She had been living in the Void and had been totally unaware of it, but now she was aware of a whole new reality.

SOMETIMES people get so involved in their work that they really don't feel connected with other people. One man had been a brilliant investment counselor. When he developed a very painful back because of metastatic cancer, he refused to take much pain medicine because he didn't want anything to interfere with his ability to think clearly and to make good investment decisions. When I first met him, it was after he had canceled our appointment on three separate occasions because various business crises had occurred at the last minute that took precedence over his acquiring hospice assistance. On our first visit, he was in so much pain that we both stood up for the interview.

He said that his pain was better if he was standing or lying flat, but that it was excruciating when he was sitting. Hence, his pattern was to get up in the morning, eat standing with the food on his chest-high dresser, tolerate an excruciatingly painful fifteen-minute drive to the office, stand up all day while using his computer placed on a chest-high bookshelf, work with clients by telephone while standing, take the excruciating drive home at 7 P.M., eat dinner standing, and then go directly to bed. Most of his clients were not even aware that he was ill because most of his business had always been conducted by phone. Although he had extensive back disease, his mind was totally un-affected and was as sharp as ever.

Of course, it was difficult to concentrate because of the pain. When I discussed options for pain control with him as we each leaned on our side of the chest of drawers, he agreed to aspirin-related medicine for his bone pain so that his mind wouldn't be affected at all, but refused anything stronger. He acknowledged that he was in agony, but said that he had to keep working.

Usually interviews are conducted both with the patient privately and with the family present as well, but this man refused to have family members present; he felt that this was his problem, not theirs. He had been divorced years ago and had had no contact with his ex-wife for years, but his adult son did live in town. When his son was contacted later by the social worker, he said that that was how his dad had always lived his life; it had been very difficult to be his son because he had always been too busy to be available for any father/son activities. It didn't surprise him that his father was too busy for his own death!

Over the next several weeks, the investment counselor gradually grew weaker, which made it more difficult for him to stand up all day. Because of the weakness, he gradually decreased his hours at work, much to his chagrin. One day he discovered that the weakness had grown so intense that he could no longer get out of bed without assistance. When his nurse arrived after his call from the bedside telephone, he was frustrated, angry, and somewhat confused.

It was obvious that he was entering into the last few days of his life. Because he no longer had the strength to get out of bed, he agreed to go to the hospice facility for help with his pain and confusion. When he first arrived there, he was combative and angry, striking out at people both physically and verbally. After a small amount of medicine for pain and anxiety, he relaxed a little, but was still quite agitated when I got there.

When I went into his room, he recognized me even in his confusion since we had leaned across the chest of drawers on several occasions. He said that he wanted a "moment of quietude" with me and asked that everyone else leave. Although he had struck out at several people in the last few minutes, there was something in his eyes that looked to me as though he wouldn't harm me and that he needed to talk about his situation. I sat down next to him and waited for him to begin. He didn't say anything for a moment or two as he tried to calm himself and gather his thoughts.

Then he looked me full in the eyes and quietly asked, "I'm dying, aren't I?" I nodded in agreement. Over the next few minutes, he talked about how he hadn't expected it to come to this. He hadn't expected to have a period of time when he would be too weak to get to the office and too unclear to make economic decisions. He recalled the times that he had changed the subject when I had tried to talk about the possibility of his not being able to continue working. Finally, he said with resignation, "Okay, this is the way that it is," and dismissed me for that day.

Over the next few days as he declined, he would call his secretary in periods of confusion and give her orders; most of what he said to her was unintelligible, but it was obvious that work was still on his mind. Whenever his son visited him, he was still distracted and muttering about work. With the support of the social worker, the son understood that he needed to see his dad for his own grief work, but that the barriers that his father had erected in health might not be lowered by his impending death. Indeed, his dad fell into an unresponsive state, still muttering about stocks and bonds. He died a few days later, having never regained consciousness. His son was his only visitor during those last days of his life. It felt to me as though he had experienced the Void right here in this lifetime.

➵ ONE young man was furious when he was diagnosed with advanced cancer. He was only thirty years old and had done everything to stay healthy—including working out five times a week and eating a low-fat diet. He had just been promoted to professional engineer and was very proud of his new home, lovely wife, and only son. He had experienced twinges of pain for several months before seeking medical attention, but had attributed the pain to the punishing work-outs that he did on a regular basis. When the cancer was discovered, there was little hope of a complete cure. In spite of aggressive treatment over the next several months, the cancer continued to advance.

Along with the advancing disease, he had increasing pain, but he refused to take enough medicines to help with the pain. He also became increasingly angry and controlling with his family. He had always led a rigid, structured life, but his response to the chaos and uncertainty of the advancing disease was to become even more controlling and rigid with his family. That felt to him like one area in his life that he could control. His wife wanted to be helpful to him, but she was really torn when he screamed at their small son for making noise and insisted on having everything in its place at all times—a virtual impossibility with a pre-schooler.

At first, he refused medicines because he felt that someone had to stay in control of the family; as he grew weaker, he refused them because the pain made him know that he was alive. He had always been a very active man and equated movement with life. He seemed to burn with the anger and the pain. No one could touch him physically because it hurt too much to be touched, and no one could touch him with a word because he would hurl anger back at them. He gradually died in pain and in anger, having never allowed anyone to really connect with him. He chose the Void instead of the Link that would have connected him with other people.

⊰ IN contrast, many families filled with rage and bitter memories from years before take the dying process as an opportunity to heal the old injuries. It is common for someone in the last few days of life to request the presence of a relative or childhood friend, for example, whom they haven't spoken to in years: They don't want to die without healing that rift.

The healing process sometimes occurs even when the dying person is no longer conscious. One person lay close to death for several days and everyone wondered why she hadn't died yet. When her husband was asked about it, he said that she and her sister had argued some twenty years ago and hadn't spoken since. After our conversation, her husband made a few phone calls and finally located her sister in another state. When she heard that her sister was dying, she, too, wanted to heal the rift. She flew into town immediately. When she arrived at her sister's side, there was no outward hint of recognition because the patient was comatose; but she died peacefully ten minutes later. It did feel as though the two sisters had reconnected at some level.

Understanding the Void has profound implications as to how we live our lives. If we are unaware of the Void and the deep sense of separation and isolation that it brings, it is very possible to live a life that brings us closer to it without even realizing what we are doing. Much of our modern world is geared toward *doing,* not toward *being.* When we fill our lives with activities and with work, we often don't leave time for being with ourselves or with other people in any deep and meaningful way. We fill our days with meaningless activities that keep us from thinking and feeling at a deeper level.

If we are angry with someone, for example, we often bury the feeling and avoid the person, thus effectively breaking our connection with them. Every time we do that we make one more break in the link of love and one more step toward the ultimate separation—the Void. When a spouse seeks comfort after a bad day at the office and we dismiss her because we're working at the computer, another link is broken, another step is taken toward this Void. When a child asks how a caterpillar becomes a butterfly and we don't take the time to answer because we "need" to mow the lawn just then—one more link is broken, one step is taken toward the Void. When we turn our heads as we walk past a bag lady, we are forgetting our connection with all people. Thus, moment by moment we choose the directions that are lives are taking.

If we were to agree that living a life of love and connection is our main goal, we would change many things in our society. First and foremost, we would simplify our lives. We would not clutter our lives with things that we don't need, thereby simultaneously releasing ourselves from the need to work hard to get those things and from the work involved in maintaining them once we get them. We would not be in a perpetual buying mode, but would seriously consider purchases as to the use they really serve in our lives and the energy, time, and money it takes to have them.

We wouldn't watch television just to occupy our time and minds, but would limit its use to specific activities that are well-considered. We wouldn't fill our days with meaningless activities that don't bring us joy. We wouldn't fill our minds with lists of inconsequential things to do, nor would we dwell on old injuries and small slights.

We would, instead, live simple lives with space and time for stillness and for deep connection. Without a lot of noise and busyness, we would begin to be more aware of our own rhythms and feelings. Knowing ourselves better, we would then be able to be more fully present with our families and our friends. Conversations would take on deeper levels beyond the superficiality of gossip and one-upmanship. Having simplified our lives, we would then have the time and energy to connect with other people in making our world a healthier, safer place for nature and for humans.

We will have deliberately moved away from the Void and toward connection. Practicing love will have become our main goal and our main joy as well. We will have learned the lesson that the Void is here to teach us.

CHAPTER 13

The Meaning of the Hospice Experience

⇥ THE previous chapter discussed the few negative NDEs that I have heard. Those did not include suicide attempts, because the NDEs that occurred during suicide attempts that were told to me were of a more positive nature. The people who had made the suicide attempt were clear on one point, however: Suicide is not an appropriate way to end a life. They felt that it just isn't in the order of things to commit suicide, no matter how difficult things are. These were universally people who were not terminally ill, but who had felt overwhelmed by their life's circumstances. I don't know if that message would change for terminally ill people or not.

The other negative aspect of the dying process is in the physical realm. It has been the general assumption among physicians and lay people, alike, that dying is a painful process. Hospice has made a big difference in that assumption. When people are dying from painful processes such as cancer, it is not a peaceful time for them if their pain is not controlled. That point was well illustrated in the previous chapter by the examples of the men who refused pain medication because of their anger and their need to be in control. That refusal kept them physically miserable, which added to their emotional misery. It is absolutely essential that people's symptoms be dealt with in a timely and careful manner if they are going to be able to devote their minds and souls to the process of finishing up business and preparing for death.

Another aspect of physical care that deserves attention is the matter of restricting movement as little as possible. It is essential that people be tied down as little as possible, so that they can feel free to go between both worlds. Many of the procedures done to people in the hospital setting, however, result in a restriction of movement.

Intravenous tubes, for example, which are used for some medications and sometimes for nutrition, result in restricted movement in the arm to which the tube is attached. Even though the tube is attached to a bag which is placed on a stand on wheels so that patients can take it with them if they are well enough to walk, it is still one more encumbrance. Catheters are often placed in the bladder to help it empty. They, too, are attached to a bag that can be carried when a person is moving about.

Frequently oxygen is attached by tubes or a mask to the nose. The tubing leads to the oxygen which comes through a tube in the wall or through a large tank. The tank isn't carried, but the person can move about if he or she is careful with the tube coming from the tank. If oxygen requirements increase, a tube may even be inserted through the nose or the mouth and into the lungs so that a respirator can breathe for them. If that happens, patients are confined to being on their backs constantly.

If vomiting becomes a problem, a tube is often inserted through the nose and threaded into the stomach. It is then attached to a wall suction machine. Hence, it is not uncommon for a person to have a tube in their nose, a mask over their nose, a tube in their arm, and a tube in their bladder. Each movement is accompanied by the sensation of a tube pulling on some part of the body, and each tube is attached to a bag or a tank. It is difficult not to focus on the body with all of these tubes tugging on different body parts!

Sometimes the tubes are absolutely necessary, but they should be confined to a bare minimum in the dying patient. Hospices frequently give medications through a subcutaneous pump which gives much more freedom of movement than the large intravenous tubes, bags, and stands. The medication is slowly delivered through a two-teaspoon syringe by means of a battery-driven pump about the size of a pack of cigarettes. People can put the syringe and pump in a pocket and go about their usual activities, free of all encumbrances. Many people have worked and shopped and visited with friends without people being aware that they have any medication being administered at all.

The same is true for people who are incontinent. There are small leg bags that can be attached by a Velcro strap under the slacks or skirt so that the person can be free to walk about with both arms free and no outward evidence of having a catheter in place. This attention to detail can allow people to be mobile longer and can allow them to be more comfortable when they are too weak to get out of bed.

When people are kept physically comfortable by controlling symptoms and minimizing encumbrances, it is remarkable how little physical discomfort they have during the last few days of life—even with terminal cancer. In the hundreds of patients that I have cared for during my hospice work, only a handful appeared uncomfortable to me in any way at the time of their death. In discussing this with other hospice workers, I learned that is their general perception as well.

Pain is nearly always controlled unless there is a catastrophic event at the end—such as a ruptured internal organ, or occasionally, intense nerve involvement. The more common difficult symptom is secretions. Although current medications control symptoms in the vast majority of people, occasionally the secretions or pain may overpower the medications.

Sometimes people are concerned about taking narcotic medications because they fear that they will be too sleepy and miss out on the last days of their lives. My experience has been quite different. People in severe pain are often so distracted that they can't think of anything but their pain. Frequently, a person who begins taking pain medications becomes, to their surprise, much more coherent than they had been for days or weeks. Without their pain screaming for attention,they are now free to focus on other matters. A word of caution, however: People do often become more confused and sleepy after *increasing* pain medication, but those symptoms usually resolve after two or three days. In fact, I have seen people on large doses of narcotic medications who were still able to go to work—although they weren't allowed to drive there themselves, of course, for safety reasons. It is very important that pain be relieved in dying patients so that they can focus on completing their life's work.

One young mother lamented the fact that she hurt so much that she couldn't be really present when her young teen-aged daughter wanted to talk about her problems. She knew that she wouldn't be there to watch her daughter grow up, and she didn't want to miss the time that she did have by being so distracted. We worked on the pain medication together with my increasing it gradually and her giving me feedback as we looked for just the right amount to take her pain away—not a drop more than she needed. She was sleepy the first few days and needed to be reminded that this was temporary while her body was adjusting to the medication and we were changing the amounts on a daily basis.

Ten days after we started our intensive work together, she greeted me with a huge smile. The day before, after her daughter had told her a story from school, her daughter looked at her and said, "Mom, it's so good to have you back."

For the next few weeks, while her daughter was at school, she thought of all of the things that she would like to be able to say to her as she matured into a young woman and finally into a mother herself. She wrote her letter after letter to be opened on special occasions such as her first day in high school, her first date, her sixteenth birthday, her graduation day, her wedding day, and on the birth of her first child. She poured in all of the love and wisdom that her thirty-five years on this Earth had given her.

When she finished the letters, she knew that she had done everything she could to be as present for her daughter as she could—even though she knew that her body would not survive until her daughter had become a young woman. Without the constant presence of the pain, the mother/daughter relationship was restored and their last days together were very meaningful ones.

❧ FREQUENTLY, people have "terminal restlessness." This is a term employed in the hospice to describe the restlessness that occurs as people begin the dying process. Most people feel at least some unease as they begin to become aware that they will be dying soon.

The unease can be helped enormously by a peaceful environment that allows them to rest in quiet without noisy corridors or being awakened at 2 A.M. to check vital signs. Sometimes quiet music is helpful. The social worker is available for counseling if they want to review their lives or, perhaps, to create a tape for their loved ones. The chaplain is available for spiritual discussions, if that is what is needed to help with the restlessness. People are encouraged to heal any remaining relationship issues, particularly those that center around the need for forgiveness. Their physical comfort is considered with gentle massages and a variety of pillows to support weak areas and ease any discomfort. Sometimes some anxiety medication is useful, as well—not to "dope" them and keep them from completing their work here, but to "take the edge off" so that they can do the work with greater equanimity.

Holding on to the body is not the focus of the team effort, but helping the person to gently let go of the body is. Symptoms are controlled so that the body and its needs slip quietly into the background, while the spiritual self emerges. One woman said, "I'm more spirit than body now," a few days before her peaceful death.

A woman who had been quite anxious all of her life became even more anxious as she felt herself nearing death. She had several adult children who lived in the same block that she did. As she became more anxious, she manifested that anxiety by asking them to do more things. They were, of course, eager to be helpful and in short order the home became a place of chaos—with six people running around waiting on a very anxious lady who didn't know what she wanted except not to feel the way that she was feeling. Unfortunately, each time that she asked for an extra pillow or an extra glass of water or to have the television set turned up or turned down, the change in the environment and the constant movement only added to her anxiety and, subsequently, to her children's anxiety as well. When the nurse arrived at their home, they were all at their wit's end and ready for a break.

This woman was transferred to the hospice unit, where everyone was experienced in dealing with anxiety and things were quiet. To help her calm down somewhat, only one or two family members were present at a time at first. Small doses of anti-anxiety medicine were given to her. A volunteer sat in the room so that she would see someone if she opened her eyes. Quiet music was played. Pillows were given to add to her comfort level, but they weren't adjusted constantly. Gradually over the next couple of hours, she was able to relax.

By the next day, she had definitely broken the cycle of anxiety and was able to visit with her large family again without becoming highly anxious. She was taught to take slow, easy breaths when she felt herself beginning to become anxious. In a couple of days, she was able to go home and was mostly anxiety-free until her death at home a few days later with her family around her saying the Twenty-third Psalm.

⇥ THE goals of hospice work with terminally-ill patients are in strong contrast to the goals of an acute care hospital, where keeping the patient alive at all costs is the main goal. The latter frequently involves great pain to the patient, with multiple procedures. Without knowing what to anticipate, patients are often in a state of confusion and terror as they wonder what painful procedures are to follow.

Furthermore, the sad fact is that most people have been dying in intensive care units where they have been transferred as they deteriorated, so that more procedures appear necessary and more tubes are required. Once in the ICU, they often see family members for fifteen-minute segments two or three times per day. Closure on relationship issues is almost impossible in that setting of scheduled short visits with the dying person in pain, terror, and confusion. Is it any wonder that people tend to see dying as a painful, terrifying process?

My plea is for physicians to be honest with patients about their medical condition and for patients to have the courage to say "No more!" when in their hearts they know the ultimate outcome. So much important soul work can be done in those last few days and hours of life that it should not be wasted in an ICU trying to live for a few more hours or days. One story will illustrate this point.

A woman had been in the ICU for several days with tubes in her veins, a tube in her stomach, a tube in her bladder, and a tube in her nose. She didn't speak English and was incredibly afraid. She had very poor short-term memory, so that as soon as her family explained to her in her native tongue why she had each tube, she would forget before they could come back again during the next visiting time several hours later. In her fear and confusion, she constantly pulled at the tubes in her veins, her nose, her stomach, and her bladder. In order not to have to keep putting the tubes back in, the nursing staff had tied her arms and legs to the sides of the bed so that she couldn't get the tubes out. The ties were not tight and they were padded, but they added to the restricted movement and the terror that she already felt.

When it was clear that she was dying in spite of all medical intervention, the family asked that she be moved to the hospice unit. Once there, all of the tubes were removed except for the oxygen. Without the tubes, the restraints were no longer necessary and those, too, were removed. With assistance, she went to the bathroom. Then she settled into her bed with her family around her, all speaking in her native tongue. In the peace and love of her family, she was able to relax. She died peacefully within the hour without restraints and in no apparent discomfort. No new medications were added at all. It appeared as though she needed a few moments of peace and quiet so that she could relax into death.

This situation is extremely common, whether people speak English or not. In fact, it is *so* common that I encourage physicians to transfer patients to hospice when no more active treatment will be undertaken, regardless of how little time they think remains in that patient's life. It is so valuable to be surrounded by family in a peaceful place, no matter how long the time is, that it is never "a waste of time."

If there is a good chance of recovery, ICUs are the perfect place to be; but they are not good places to die. For that reason, the new emphasis on "Advance Medical Directives" is so important. By completing an "Advance Medical Directive," people specify before they are ill whether or not they want resuscitation or intubation if there is no reasonable chance of recovery. In that way, they retain control over their lives even if they aren't conscious; they don't have to wait for family members to decide those issues. Neither do they place the responsibility on family members, but retain it for themselves, where it rightfully belongs.

We do each have our own views on these subjects. It would be good for families to have frank discussions with one another so that they all know what the other family members want. Then they can be respectful of one another's wishes even in the event of an accident or catastrosphic illness that prohibits discussion at the time of the event. A discussion like that also opens that family to a wider discussion of the meaning of life and, perhaps, a greater connection to and understanding of one another.

Without having discussed wishes in advance, family members often insist that a person be kept alive at all costs and thereby rob that person of the opportunity to die with dignity and grace. They aren't sure what to do, so they allow all possible procedures to be done to their loved one—thus ensuring a more painful death. If the discussion had been held ahead of time, they could rest assured that they were carrying out their loved ones wishes and spend their last time together in unity and in peace.

In summary, from my point of view, negative experiences are by far the exception rather than the rule in the hospice context and in NDEs. We can each only tell the truth as we see it. I encourage people to share all of their experiences, recognizing that we are each part of the whole and none of us is separate. What impacts one of us impacts us all. Only by sharing our experiences can we come to a greater understanding of the deeper mysteries of life.

CHAPTER 14

Conclusions

◈ AFTER talking with hundreds of people in the past several years, I am convinced that contact with alternate realities is the rule rather than the exception. Sometimes that contact takes the form of a near-death experience. More often, however, it occurs in the normal course of a person's life, when they are physically well.

It may occur as the result of a determined search for the mystical. It may occur during a time of tremendous mental and emotional upheaval. Or, like Paul's experience on the road to Damascus as described in the New Testament, it may occur in the midst of ordinary activities. In our modern technological society, we are so conditioned to continually manipulating our physical environment that the idea that much of life is beyond the physical may seem very strange. However, a wealth of studies testifies that it is not strange at all.

Studies on the effect of prayer on healing, for example, have shown that people heal faster when they are prayed for, even if they don't know that they are the objects of the prayers. In a study reported in the *Southern Medical Journal* by Dr. Randolph Byrd, patients recovering from open-heart surgery in an ICU were assigned randomly to one of two groups: one was prayed for, the other was not.[11] All of the patients received appropriate modern medical care. Neither the physicians involved nor the patients themselves knew who was in which group. When the recovery process was evaluated, the people who had been prayed for had fewer complications and were discharged from the hospital sooner than the people who received similar medical care but were not prayed for. Certainly, the much-maligned "placebo" effect was not in play here, since the patients didn't know that they were the recipients of prayers.

The "placebo effect" itself is a well-known fact in medicine. When patients are given a pill that contains no medication, but are told that it will make them well, a significant proportion of people will get well. The "placebo effect" is so powerful that all drug companies include a double blind-study when they are testing a new medication. A double blind-study means that neither the patient receiving the medication nor the physician administering it knows whether the patient is receiving the medication being tested or a placebo (an inert substance). There is always some effect from the placebo (either in healing or in perceived side-effects); this factor is subtracted from the effect of the medication to determine how helpful the medication will be in the medical condition being treated and to see the side-effect profile of the proposed medication.

The "placebo effect" is generally considered a nuisance factor in traditional medicine, but what a powerful statement it makes about the effect of our mind and emotions on the state of our physical health and symptoms! When someone is healed after taking a placebo, it is that person's own mind that does the healing, not the physical effect of a medicine. Yet the mainstream western medical community has only recently begun to study seriously the power of the mind in healing.

Another fascinating study of the effects of the nonphysical on human behavior was done by the Maharishi Institute in Iowa. A group of experienced meditators focused on peace in the Middle East during a time of daily skirmishes. On the days that their attention was focused in this way, there were fewer casualties and fewer outbursts of violence. This was demonstrated on several occasions and was presented in a graph by Dr. John Hagelin, a physicist from the Institute, at a conference in 1991.[12] Of course, the troops in the Middle East had no idea that they were receiving the focused attention of the meditators.

Had they known, they probably would have been quite surprised that their actions could be influenced by meditators half-way around the world!

In near-death experiences, people often describe something that was occurring in a location outside of the room where they were undergoing the experience. I have heard people describe specific conversations that were occurring in a hospital waiting room while they were being resuscitated in a place two or three floors away. Furthermore, people have told me that they were aware of what resuscitators were thinking during the resuscitation. To the embarrassment of the resuscitators, these thoughts often had nothing to do with the patient, even during a cardiopulmonary resuscitation.

Physical reality as we currently understand it doesn't explain the frequent experiences of people feeling "guided" to take a different route on the freeway and, thereby, narrowly missing a terrible accident. Calling it a hunch doesn't explain how a person knows it in the first place. Scientists have no explanation for such phenomena.

These are just a few wide-ranging examples of various ways that alternate realities impinge on our lives in a very concrete way. The less concrete impingements may be of even greater significance, but they are less dramatic to the skeptic who wants to see things in a physical way. To the person having the experience, however, they are extraordinarily powerful.

Many people have shared profound mystical experiences with me that they have told to only one or two other people in their lives. My sense from all of this has been that most people probably have at least one mystical experience in their lives, though they may try to dismiss it as a "weird dream" or may intentionally ignore its meaning. Because we are not sharing these experiences with each other, there is the sense that mystical experiences are not common.

Few people have the courage of Paul in the New Testament, who went forth from the moment that he encountered the shining light and changed his entire lifestyle, belief system, and, even his name. That called for a complete reversal of all that had gone before. It is often easier to repress the experience than to deal with it.

As mentioned earlier, it seems that people can repress a mystical experience that occurs in the course of ordinary life more easily than they can repress one that occurs during an NDE. This may be because the NDE is a deeper experience. Or it may be that the physical changes inherent in whatever brought on the NDE remind a person of his or her mortality, which makes it easier for them to restructure their thinking at that point in life. It may also be that the physical problem that precipitated the NDE requires the person to be still and avoid unnecessary activities, thus allowing time to contemplate the experience. An NDE is a unique combination of a profound physical experience and a profound mystical experience that allows profound changes in one's view of the world.

⇥ PEOPLE in the last few days of life are also in the unique position of being in two worlds at once. While their physical world is declining, their spiritual world is becoming more active. I have frequently observed that as people become more comfortable physically, with their pain controlled by medications, their minds become clearer because they are not so distracted by their pain. When their bodies are no longer screaming for attention, they can then focus on their interior life. It is then that they most often have profoundly meaningful experiences that help them to heal all that needs to be healed on this plane and prepare for their deaths.

What usually needs to be healed is their relationships. Sometimes people with young children also have financial concerns that are paramount in the last few days of life, but it is primarily relationships in need of forgiveness that I see come up again and again. Often the "unfinished business" involves estrangements that arose years ago and have been repressed until the final days. It is so common for comatose patients to wait to die until an estranged loved one arrives that, when someone has lingered longer than appears medically possible, we ask family members if there might be someone they are waiting to see before they die. Frequently, it is a long-term estrangement. If we can find the person, often their mere presence is enough to allow the patient to die in peace, even though they never wake up and never say a word. Death usually comes within minutes or hours after the arrival of that person. Here is another example of an alternate reality that affects the physical world, and the deep-seated need for forgiveness in relationships.

Sometimes it is difficult for people to allow themselves to die because the family members are so attached to them. One mother was distraught because her teen-aged daughter was dying of cancer. She sat by her side with tears streaming down her face and readily told everyone that she would do anything to keep her daughter alive as long as possible. After several days, the grief-stricken mother began to soften her resolve. Finally, she was able to say to her daughter that it was okay for her to die. Her daughter took one breath and died peacefully. It was as if she remained long enough for her mother to be able to let her go.

In that same vein, several people in my care have died when family members stepped outside for a moment or two. It was as if, at some level, they wanted to die alone or to save the family members the experience of being present at their deaths. It is important for people to be aware of this phenomenon, because they often feel guilty about stepping outside the room, however briefly.

Sometimes a dying person has just one more thing to do. One mother lay dying in a hospital setting. She was extremely weak and had been "seeing" deceased relatives for days when she begged to go home. The family had been visiting her, but hadn't brought her toddler because he was too young to enter the hospital. As soon as she got home, she asked to hold her son once more. She was too weak to support him entirely, but her husband helped her hold him while she kissed him once more. After a moment or two, she said, "Thank you," and drifted into a sleep from which she did not awaken. She died a few hours later, having summoned all her energy to say "good-bye" to her only child. It is important to listen to the wishes of a dying patient: Only they know what they need and what will bring them peace and release.

Another fascinating thing that frequently occurs in dying patients is their foreknowledge of when their deaths will occur. One man told his family on Saturday that he would die on Thursday. Although he had terminal cancer, he was expected to live weeks to months. He had no new symptoms or any discomfort, so medications were not changed. Two days later, he began to become less responsive. As he fell into a semi-comatose state, he asked his wife if it was Thursday yet. She told him that it was Monday and he slipped into an unresponsive state, from which he never awakened. He died three days later on Thursday morning.

Although that date did not seem particularly significant to him, it is quite common for people who are terminally ill to hold on for a few days or weeks for an important event such as a wedding, a wedding anniversary, or a birthday. I remember one wonderful mother of several children who remained very close to death for several days until the day after her youngest child celebrated his twenty-first birthday. It felt to me that she held on until her job was entirely finished, and then she felt ready to let go.

A man remained close to death for several days until the day that the insurance policy which ensured that his wife would be financially cared for took effect. Again, he was unresponsive, and our current scientific knowledge does not account for his knowing time in that state. Perhaps it was more of a deep connection with his wife, who was certainly aware of the time and very relieved that he lived until the insurance policy became effective.

Another example of a deep connection between spouses occurred in a couple in their seventies. They had been very close for many years. As she lay dying from cancer, he held her hand and lay his head next to her on the bed. They stayed like this for some time in close communication, and then he found himself starting to go down a tunnel. He was still holding her hand as she led the way. At that moment, the nurse touched his shoulder and told him that his wife had just died. Perhaps the shared near-death experience is a tribute to how very close these two people felt to each other. It was definitely simultaneous with her death, as witnessed by the nurse. It is also definitely something that can't be explained by ordinary physical reality as we currently understand it.

⇥ AS people become more comfortable with sharing experiences of alternate realities with each other, I envision the nonphysical gaining an important place in our understanding of how the world works. My firm conviction is that the physical has seemed so paramount because we have refused, by cultural agreement, to discuss or see the non-physical. As that agreement breaks down and people begin sharing their experiences, the greater breadth of how the world functions will begin to become more apparent. We will see that we are all much more interconnected than we have heretofore thought. We will see how much our thoughts and emotions affect one another.

As people have learned who have had a life review during an NDE, we will understand that our purpose in life is to learn how to love one another in every circumstance and in every encounter. As we begin to incorporate that truth into our knowledge of how the world functions, we will begin to accept the goal of being loving and kind in every moment as a cultural norm. When that is the cultural norm, the person who behaves unkindly will be considered deviant.

It will no longer be the norm to attack people for holding different belief systems. War will be obsolete. It will no longer be appropriate to approach others with a "chip on your shoulder." It will no longer be the norm to consider your ethnic and/or religious group as the only "in" group. It will be understood that we are all interconnected and that love is the link that connects us all— not color or creed.

With this new understanding of our purpose here, I envision a world in which cooperation and caring can solve our environmental and scarcity problems with ease, as we each contribute our skills and resources to the problems. When we are no longer hoarding skills and resources for ourselves, there will be enough to go around. When we understand that we are here to learn to be more loving, we will require fewer physical objects and will prefer life-enhancing activities to expensive entertainment that keeps us from being present with ourselves. Our greatest joy will be to be fully present with ourselves and with other people. Our own interests will no longer be more paramount to us than the interests of our neighbors.

We will then have returned to the Garden of Eden and it will be a garden of the Spirit, whose main crop is love.

REFERENCES

1. Ring, Kenneth. 1984. *Heading Toward Omega*. New York: William Morrow.

2. *A Course in Miracles*. 1975. Tiburon, CA: Foundation for Inner Peace.

3. Sabom, Michael, M.D. 1982. *Recollections of Death*. New York: Harper and Row.

4. Moody, Raymond, M.D. 1975, *Life After Life* (New York: Bantam, published by arrangement with Mockingbird Books.

5. Greyson, Bruce. "Varieties of Near-Death Experiences." *Psychiatry* 1993 Nov; 56(4), 390–9.

6. Kubler-Ross, Elisabeth, M.D. 1969. *On Death and Dying*. New York: Macmillan Publishing Co.

7. Benson, Herbert, M.D. 1990. Comments from lecture presented in Danvers, Mass. in October, 1990 at Health and Spirituality Conference. Unpublished.

8. Greyson, Bruce, M.D. 1981. "Near-Death Experiences and Attempted Suicide." *Suicide and Life-Threatening Behavior,* vol. 11, 10–16.

9. Morse, Melvin, M.D. 1990. *Closer to the Light*. New York: Villard Books.

10. Gallup, George, Jr. with William Proctor. 1982. *Adventures in Immortality: A Look Beyond the Threshold of Death*. New York: McGraw-Hill.

11. Byrd, Randolph, M.D. 1988. "Positive Therapeutic Effects of Intercessory Prayer in a Coronary Care Unit Population." *Southern Medical Journal* 81:7 (July): 826–29.

12. Hagelin, John, Ph.D. Comments from lecture presented at Isthmus Institute 1991 Conference: "Can Consciousness Survive Physical Death?" Dallas, Texas.

Of Related Interest

VISIONS OF GOD
FROM THE
NEAR DEATH EXPERIENCE

by Ken R. Vincent

"A fine, useful, and enlightening volume."
—Dr. Raymond A. Moody

*"For persons short on time or energy who need
to get straight to 'the good stuff,' this book is
it—there's nothing else like it available. It would
be a wonderful gift for anyone faced with imminent death or in bereavement. Many others
will read it just to get the 'spiritual hits' these
inspiring near death narratives provide."*
—Dr. Kenneth Ring

*"Visions is wonderful. I love it very much.
Congratulations to Ken Vincent."*
—Elisabeth Kubler-Ross

168 pages • 5-1/2 x 8-1/2
0-943914-66-3, $18.95 cloth • 0-943914-67-1, $11.95 quality paperback

Available in fine bookstores and direct from Larson Publications.
For more information call 607-546-9342 or write Larson Publications,
4936 Route 414, Burdett, NY 14818. For MC/VISA orders only:
1-800-828-2197, 9am-5pm EST.